THIS BOOK BELONGS TO

. . . . . . . . . . . . . . . . . . . . . . . . . . . . .

*To Sebastian with love. Grow up wild, curious and full of joy.*
**E.J.**

*For Charlie, who loves sea swimming as much as I do –*
*thanks for inventing 'It's a Rubbish Game!'*

**A.W.**

First published 2022 by Nosy Crow Ltd.
The Crow's Nest, 14 Baden Place, Crosby Row, London SE1 1YW, UK

Nosy Crow Eireann Ltd
44 Orchard Grove, Kenmare, Co Kerry, V93 FY22, Ireland

www.nosycrow.com

ISBN 978 1 83994 538 0

'The National Trust' and the oak leaf logo are registered trademarks of The National Trust
(Enterprises) Limited (a subsidiary of The National Trust for Places of
Historic Interest or Natural Beauty, Registered Charity Number 205846)

Nosy Crow and associated logos are trademarks and/or registered trademarks of Nosy Crow Ltd.

Text © Anna Wilson 2018, 2019, 2020, 2021, 2022
Illustrations © Elly Jahnz 2018, 2019, 2020, 2021, 2022

The right of Anna Wilson to be identified as the author and Elly Jahnz
to be identified as the illustrator of this work has been asserted.

A CIP catalogue record for this book is available from the British Library.

Printed in China

Papers used by Nosy Crow are made from wood grown in sustainable forests.

1 3 5 7 9 8 6 4 2

National Trust

# 2023 NATURE MONTH-BY-MONTH

## A Children's Almanac

Anna Wilson     Elly Jahnz

Nosy Crow

# WHAT IS AN ALMANAC?

The first almanacs were created about 3,000 years ago! They were written by the ancient Egyptians, who used a kind of paper made from reeds known as papyrus. The writers listed all the dates that were thought to be lucky or unlucky, and made predictions about the weather. Farmers used these almanacs to help them know when to plant seeds and when to harvest crops.

Nowadays you can also find almanacs (like this one!) which have fun facts about each month – things to do indoors and outdoors, animals to spot, festivals to celebrate and seasonal food to grow, cook and eat. They also contain information about the weather, the night sky and all sorts of other amazing facts.

## WARNING!

This book contains activities which involve things like knives, saws, hammers and nails and hot ovens. There are also a lot of fun things to do outside which involve fire and very cold water! All the activities are safe if you are sensible, follow safety guidelines and take a grown-up along to look out for you.

# CONTENTS

# JANUARY

## SPECIAL DAYS

**1st** New Year's Day/First-footing
**5th** Twelfth Night/Wassailing
**6th** Epiphany
**13th** Lohri (Punjabi midwinter festival)
**22nd** Chinese New Year (Year of the Rabbit)
**25th** Burns Night

# ANNIVERSARIES

### 75 years ago . . .

On 12 January 1948, the London Co-operative Society opened Britain's first self-service supermarket in Manor Park, London. Before then, you couldn't help yourself to things from the shelves – you had to ask a shopkeeper for what you wanted.

### 160 years ago . . .

On 10 January 1863, the London Underground was opened. The Metropolitan Railway was the first line on the Underground. It ran for 6 kilometres between Farringdon Street and Bishop's Road, Paddington.

### 250 years ago . . .

On 17 January 1773, Captain James Cook and his crew became the first Europeans to sail below the Antarctic Circle.

_"January brings the snow,_
_Makes our feet and fingers glow."_

SARA COLERIDGE (1802–1852)

January can be a dull and dreary month after the excitement of Christmas and New Year's Eve – unless it snows of course! Who doesn't love a 'snow day'? Even if it doesn't snow, there are still lots of lovely things you can do, both outdoors and indoors, this month. You could wrap up warm and go for a walk to see what you can find. Yes, the trees are bare, but you should still be able to spot birds and other creatures out in the park or garden. There are also some wonderful festivals this month which offer a good excuse for getting friends round or throwing a party. So maybe January is not so dull after all!

### Why is January Called January?

The calendar we use today was invented by the Romans. January was named after the Roman god Janus, who was the god of gates and doorways. He was always drawn with two faces looking in opposite directions – one face looked back at the year that had passed, and the other looked forwards into the new year.

## DID YOU KNOW...

In the United States of America, the third Monday of January is known as Martin Luther King Day. On this day, people remember the important work Martin Luther King did to achieve equal rights for people of colour.

**New Year's Resolutions**

On 31st December we often talk about 'making resolutions' for the new year. Why do we do this?

The tradition of making resolutions started with the Romans too. Because the January god, Janus, was looking backwards and forwards at the same time, he became a symbol for the Romans of forgetting what had happened in the past and moving on into the future. January therefore became known as a month in which to forgive people and be kind.

Nowadays, people seem to worry more about getting fit and not eating chocolate – maybe we should be more like the Romans and make resolutions to be kinder instead?

Here are some ideas for resolutions that you might manage to keep . . .

- Look out for someone at school who needs a friend.
- Have a cake sale or organise a sponsored silence or a sponsored walk for charity.
- Clear out your old toys and clothes and take them to a charity shop. (Check with an adult before you give these things away!)
- Help out around the house and/or garden, if you have one.

# FESTIVAL FUN

The colourful festivals of light such as Christmas, Hanukkah and Diwali might be over, but January has its fair share of celebrations to look forward to.

### 5th January  *Twelfth Night*

Twelfth Night is a Christian festival which marks the end of the Christmas period. Sometimes it is celebrated on 5th January and sometimes on 6th January! It depends on whether you count the Christmas season as starting on 25th or 26th December.

### 5th January  *Wassailing*

Wassailing is a pagan tradition. The word *wassail* comes from the Anglo-Saxon words *waes hael* which mean 'good health'. The festival is like many other winter celebrations in that it looks forward to what people hope for in the new year to come: good weather, good health and a good harvest.

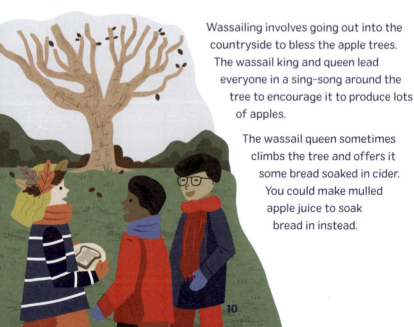

Wassailing involves going out into the countryside to bless the apple trees. The wassail king and queen lead everyone in a sing-song around the tree to encourage it to produce lots of apples.

The wassail queen sometimes climbs the tree and offers it some bread soaked in cider. You could make mulled apple juice to soak bread in instead.

**6th January** *Epiphany*

6th January is also known as Epiphany or the Feast of the Three Kings. In Britain there is an old superstition that it is unlucky to leave your Christmas decorations up after this date. In some other countries 6th January is called St Nicholas's Day, and this is the day on which children get presents instead of Christmas Day.

**13th January** *Lohri*

Hindus and Sikhs all over the world celebrate Lohri. During Lohri, songs are sung to the sun god Surya, thanking him for his warmth and praying for his return after the cold weather.

People drink *gurh* – a delicious sugary drink made from sugar cane. *Gajak* is also eaten – a thin, dry sweet made from roasted sesame seeds cooked in sugar syrup and spices. Children go from house to house singing folk songs and are given sweets. In the evening, a bonfire is lit and people gather together to dance.

**25th January**
*Burns Night*

Burns Night celebrates the birthday of Scotland's most famous poet, Robert Burns. He wrote the song 'Auld Lang Syne', which we sing on New Year's Eve. In Scotland, people have a Burns Night supper, which includes the national dish of haggis, neeps (mashed turnips) and tatties (mashed potatoes).

## 22nd January *Chinese New Year*

Chinese New Year is a noisy and colourful occasion and there will be festivities in big cities throughout Britain. There are firecrackers, lion and dragon dances, music, parades, lanterns and special foods such as noodles. People wear red clothes for luck and to ward off evil spirits.

2023 is the Year of the Rabbit, the fourth of the 12 animals in the Chinese Zodiac. In Chinese culture, people born in the Year of the Rabbit are said to be brave and active people who enjoy challenges and adventures.

### DID YOU KNOW...

The decorations for Chinese New Year are mostly all red. This is because red is considered a very lucky colour – it is the symbol for wealth and happiness and good fortune and it is believed to scare away any evil spirits. This is why red lanterns can be seen decorating the streets at this time.

## Make a *Paper Chinese Lantern*

**You will need:**

**Balloon**
**Sheets of newspaper or tissue paper**
**PVA glue**
**Red poster paint**
**Gold or yellow paint**
**Paintbrushes**
**Pin**
**Scissors**
**Skewer**
**String**
**LED tea light (optional)**

Why not make your own lantern to hang up inside? Make sure you never put a candle flame in or near the lantern. Also do not release it outside as it will float away and cause litter. When your celebrations are over, you can pack the lantern away and reuse it next year, or recycle the materials you have used.

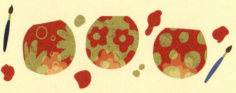

1 *Blow up the balloon to the size you want your lantern to be and tie a knot in the end.*

2 *Tear up the newspaper or tissue paper into squares of roughly 2–3 cm.*

3 *Paste the paper all over the balloon using the glue and a brush and leaving the knot free.*

4 *Leave this first layer to dry and then complete step three, four or five times.*

5 *Leave the balloon to dry out completely – overnight is best.*

6 *Once the balloon is dry, you can paint it! Remember, red is the luckiest colour, but you can decorate it with gold or yellow too, once the red paint has dried.*

7 *When the paint is all dry, you can pop the balloon inside! Ask an adult to help you to do this with a pin.*

8 *Cut the knot of the balloon with some scissors – there should be a small hole now so that you can pull the balloon out of the paper ball.*

9 *Ask an adult to help you to cut a bit more of the paper away so that you have a paper bowl.*

10 *Make two holes in the top of the bowl so that you can thread string through to hang your lantern up.*

11 *Put an LED tea light in the bottom of the bowl so that your lantern lights up safely.*

12 *Hang your lantern in your bedroom or in the window of your house so that people can see it when they walk by!*

# OUTDOOR ADVENTURES

Just as the festivals remind us that January is a month of hope and looking forward to new things, nature is doing its best to give us hope too. If you go out into the garden, the park or the woods near where you live, you will see signs of new life even on the darkest day. It depends on which area of the country you are in, of course. In the colder northern regions, plants take longer to appear, while down in the south you might see green shoots as early as 1st January.

One of the first plants that starts to peep up out of the ground this month is the snowdrop. These tiny white and green flowers might look fragile, but they can survive during the coldest weather – even with snow and ice!

Other plants are growing too: have a look at the trees next time you go on a walk. Can you see any hazel catkins? They grow long before there are any leaves on the trees.

And then there are all the animals and birds to look out for. Squirrels are about, trying to remember where they buried their nuts and seeds in the autumn! Have a look for birds building their nests too – it may seem early, but blue tits and coal tits are very busy collecting twigs and feathers and fur for their nests. If you do find a nest, don't touch it even if it looks old – birds will not come back and lay their eggs there if a human has disturbed it.

**Make a** *Nature Notebook*

1  *Take some sheets of scrap paper, fold them in half to make a booklet, then staple them together where you've made the fold.*

2  *Remember to make the notebook small enough to fit into a pocket so you can take it with you wherever you go.*

3  *Tie a piece of string to a pencil and stick the loose end of the string into the notebook with sticky tape or make a hole in the pages and thread the string through. Use the pencil to note down where and when you see things while you are out and about.*

CAN YOU SPOT...

Primroses

Daffodils

Owl

Hazel catkins

Fox

Snowdrops

Mouse

Rabbit

# WINTER SENSES

Sometimes it's very tempting to stay snuggled up at home in January, but it's amazing how much better we feel once we have been outside for a walk. One of the best places to go to is a forest or wood where there are evergreen trees. You could try using all five of your senses while you are on your winter walk:

**1** **Sight** Look closely at the trees. Many conifer trees (such as pine, spruce and fir) grow in a spiral pattern. You can guess how old the tree is by counting the spirals, or 'whorls', because after about two years, the tree will grow a new whorl of branches each year.

**2** **Sound** Stop and listen to the noises of the forest or wood. If it's dry, you could even lie down on the ground for a bit. Can you hear the wind through the trees? Or the rustle of animals or birds? How does the ground sound when you walk on it?

**3** **Touch** Have a look around you for pine cones or dried leaves. What do they feel like? Run your fingers over a tree trunk. Do you feel excited? Happy? Calm?

**4** **Smell** Breathe in the smells around you. If you've walked here before, does the wood smell different to the last time you were here?

**5** **Taste** We can't eat the actual trees, of course! But when we smell, we use our sense of taste as well. What can you taste from the air around you?

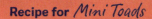

## Recipe for *Mini Toads*

When the weather outside is frightful, it's always nice to cook up something delightful! Toad-in-the-hole is an especially comforting meal as the sausages are cooked in a batter like Yorkshire pudding, so it's filling, warm and tasty. These 'mini toads' are perfect for a party or a quick and simple tea. The recipe is easy, but you'll need help getting the tin in and out of the oven.

**You will need:**

Teaspoon
Mixing bowl
Measuring jug
Scales
Whisk
12-hole muffin tin
Heatproof surface
Spatula
Oven gloves

2 tablespoons of sunflower oil
24 mini sausages or 12 chipolatas cut in half
3 large eggs
150 ml plain flour
150 ml milk
(optional)

1 *Heat the oven to 220°C/200°C fan/gas mark 6.*

2 *Put two mini sausages or two halves of a chipolata in each muffin hole.*

3 *Drizzle the sunflower oil over the sausages.*

4 *Cook in the oven for about 15 minutes until the sausages have turned brown.*

5 *While the sausages are cooking, weigh out the flour and put it in the mixing bowl.*

6 *Make a small well in the flour with your hand and crack the eggs into the dip.*

7 *Pour a little of the milk on to the eggs and start whisking, then add the rest of the milk slowly.*

8 *Keep whisking until you have a thin batter that looks like double cream.*

9 *Pour the batter into a measuring jug.*

10 *Ask an adult to get the sausages out of the oven and put the muffin tin on a heatproof surface.*

11 *Ask for help pouring the batter on top of the sizzling-hot sausages so that you fill each muffin hole about three quarters of the way up.*

12 *Put the muffin tin back in the oven and cook for another 15 minutes until the batter has risen and is golden – if your oven has a glass door you can watch the batter rise!*

13 *Take the tin out of the oven and let the 'toads' cool slightly before removing them with a spatula.*

14 *Eat them with ketchup – and mashed potato if you are really hungry! You won't feel cold and wintery now!*

# THE SEASIDE IN WINTER

Maybe a trip to the seaside is not at the top of your list of things to do at this time of year! It's true that it's too chilly to go for a swim or a paddle, as the sea temperature has dropped to between 6°C and 10°C. However, you can still have fun hunting for shells, pebbles and seaweed. And there are some beautiful seabirds and other creatures for you to spot. Common seals can be seen along the British coastline, and in Scotland, Wales and Cornwall you might also see porpoises. Wherever you go, make sure you take your home-made nature notebook with you so that you can write down or draw what you spot!

CAN YOU SPOT...

Gannet

Shag

Cormorant

Turnstone

Rock pipit

Redshank

Oystercatcher

Curlew

Take a bucket and a net with you too. The weather may not be good enough for you to sit about making sandcastles, but hopping between the rock pools will keep you warm. See how many different objects you can find. The winter storms bring in all sorts of treasures, from pretty shells to funny-shaped driftwood to sea-softened pieces of coloured glass. Have a competition with your friends and family – the person with the most items wins. If you're really lucky, you may even find some real buried treasure!

## DID YOU KNOW...

Almost three quarters of the surface of our planet is made up of the oceans. This is the reason that Earth looks blue from outer space.

# FEBRUARY

## SPECIAL DAYS

**2nd**   Imbolc (pagan celebration)/
Candlemas (Christian festival)

**6th**   Tu B'Shevat (Jewish New Year)

**14th**  St Valentine's Day

**18th**  Isra and Mi'raj (Muslim celebration)

**21st**  Shrove Tuesday (Pancake Day)

**22nd** Ash Wednesday (Christian festival)

# ANNIVERSARIES

**100 years ago . . .**

On 16 February 1923, the Egyptologist and archaeologist Howard Carter opened up the burial chamber of the pharaoh Tutankhamun. The contents of the tomb taught us a lot about how the ancient Egyptians lived.

**195 years ago . . .**

On 8 February 1828, the French author Jules Verne was born. He is famous for writing books such as *Twenty-thousand Leagues Under the Sea* and is often mentioned as one of the first writers of science fiction.

# "Late February days; and now at last, Might you have thought that Winter's woe was past."

WILLIAM MORRIS (1834–1896)

February is a short month – this year it has only 28 days. Many people think this is good, as the weather can be bad and the days are quite dark. In fact, the days start to get longer, and by the end of February we will have two hours more daylight than at the start of the month.

Spring is not far away: animals and plants are slowly waking up as nature gets ready to show off all its colours and lovely smells. Look around – what can you see peeking out of the soil? There will be plants to see out there, however small.

Many religions think of February as a quiet month in which to be still and thankful. Some hold 'fasts', which means that they do not eat during the day to help them concentrate on prayer and mindfulness. Why not try having some quiet time each day in February? It's a good way to feel grateful for things in life – especially on a cold, dark day!

## Why is February Called February?

The Latin name for this month was *Februarius*. It came from the Latin word *februum* which means 'purification'. The Romans thought of the fifth day of this month as the official first day of spring. On the 15th they celebrated a festival called *Februa*.

This was a time to get rid of evil spirits and to cleanse the air so that people felt fit and healthy for spring. This is where we get our idea of spring cleaning from. Perhaps you could use the colder, darker days this month to tidy your bedroom or help clear out the shed or garage.

## February Birth Signs

**Aquarius**  The sign of the water-carrier. Some people believe that if you have your birthday between 20th January and 18th February, then this is your sign. You are supposed to be an inquisitive and logical person.

**Pisces**  The sign of the fish. If you were born between 19th February and 20th March, then you are a Piscean. Some people believe this means you are creative and good at working things out based on your feelings.

### Birth Flower and Birthstone

Each month has a special flower and stone. February's flower is the violet. It is supposed to represent faithfulness, wisdom and hope, so anyone born in this month is said to be 'always true'. The stone is purple amethyst. The ancient Greeks believed that if you wore the stone, it would protect you from being poisoned! It is said to give you courage as well.

## DID YOU KNOW ...

The Welsh sometimes refer to February as *y mis bach* which translates as 'little month' because it is the shortest month in the year. February used to have as few as 23 days until the calendar was changed! Now it has 28 days, except in a leap year, when it has an extra day. Leap years happen every four years (apart from in the year 2000).

# FESTIVAL FUN

### 2nd February *Imbolc*

Imbolc (pronounced 'imulk') is a pagan festival. Its name comes from the Celtic word *imbolg* which means 'in the belly'. This is because nature seems to be expecting lots of babies at this time of year – baby animals, baby trees, baby flowers and fruit and vegetables. Everything is hidden away at the moment, but that doesn't mean nothing is happening deep in the cold, dark ground – or inside pregnant animals! To celebrate, people sometimes make dolls from corn called 'Bridey dolls' which are said to bring good luck.

### 2nd February *Candlemas*

Candlemas is a Christian festival. It celebrates the day that the baby Jesus was taken to the temple for the first time. The festival always takes place on 2nd February and marks the end of the Christmas season. At Ripon Cathedral in Yorkshire, people celebrate by lighting 5,000 candles to symbolise Jesus bringing light into the darkness of the world.

### 6th February *Tu B'Shevat*

Tu B'Shevat is a Jewish festival, also known as Rosh Hashanah La'Ilanot, or 'The New Year of the Trees'. Like Wassailing, it is a time to give thanks for the trees coming to life and growing new green shoots after the winter. The day is celebrated with a feast of seven foods which are found growing in Israel: wheat, barley, grapes, figs, pomegranates, olives and dates.

## Make a *Handprint Tree*

As Tu B'Shevat is a festival of trees, why not make a beautiful tree picture to celebrate how wonderful trees are.

**You will need:**

**Pencil**
**Washable finger paints – green, yellow, orange**
**Some plates**
**Paintbrushes**
**Large sheet of card or paper**
**Washing-up bowl of water**
**Some old towels**

1. *Mix together yellow and orange paint on a plate until you get the colour brown you would like for the trunk and branches.*
2. *Put the palm of your hand in the paint.*
3. *Place your palm in the middle of your paper or card and press down.*
4. *Now you have the branches!*
5. *Wash the brown paint off your hand.*
6. *Use a paintbrush and the rest of the brown paint to colour in the trunk.*
7. *Put blobs of yellow, green, orange and brown paint on another plate.*
8. *Press your finger into one of the colours and dot it over the 'branches' to make 'leaves'.*
9. *Wash your hand and choose another colour.*
10. *Do this over and over until you have lots and lots of different coloured leaves on the tree.*
11. *Put the picture aside to dry.*
12. *Hang it up on Tu B'Shevat or give it as a present to someone in your family.*

## TOP TIP

This is a messy activity! Wear an apron or art overall, and cover the table in old newspaper or a wipe-clean tablecloth.

## 14th February *St Valentine's Day*

St Valentine's Day is an ancient tradition. Today, it's seen as a day to celebrate love. People send cards and flowers (particularly red roses), chocolates and other gifts. In some parts of Norfolk and Suffolk there is an old custom of leaving presents on people's doorsteps on St Valentine's Eve, the night before St Valentine's Day.

 **Make** *Love-heart Bunting*

**You will need:**

**White paper for the template**
**Scraps of different fabrics**
**Needle and thread**
**Scissors and/or pinking shears**
**String or ribbon**
**Glue**
**Stiff card**
**Clothes pegs**

### TOP TIP

If you don't have fabric scraps at home, you can get bags of them from most fabric shops or haberdashers, or you can buy fabric 'quilting' squares. Choose as many different colours and patterns as you like, or stick to one or two designs and alternate them!

1. *Fold your white paper in half and cut half a heart shape so that when you open the paper you have a perfect loveheart. (If you want to make some hearts smaller than others you'll need to make more than one template.)*

2. *Roughly sew the template on to a piece of fabric to hold it still while you cut around it. Pinking shears make the edges look pretty, but you can use ordinary scissors too.*

3. *Ask an adult to help you sew the hearts on to a piece of ribbon, or glue them on to card to keep them stiff, then hang them on a piece of string with clothes pegs.*

4. *Hang them up around your house for Valentine's Day!*

5. *Remember to put the bunting away safely so that you can reuse it next year, or use it in the summer for a garden party or birthday celebration.*

## 18th February *Isra and Mi'raj*

This festival is in two parts. The first part, the *Isra* or the 'Night Journey', starts on the evening before the day of celebrations. Muslims remember the Prophet Muhammad's journey from Mecca to Jerusalem and then to heaven. Muslim people believe the Night Journey started when the Angel Gabriel took the Prophet Muhammad to Jerusalem on a winged horse, where he met and prayed with prophets including Moses and Jesus.

The second part is the *Mi'raj*, which means 'ladder' in Arabic. This was when the Prophet Muhammad was carried up to heaven by Gabriel where he spoke to Allah (God), who told the prophet that Muslims should say their prayers five times a day. At Isra and Mi'raj, Muslim people say prayers during the night and Muslim cities keep their lights on all night.

## 21st February *Shrove Tuesday (Pancake Day)*

Shrove Tuesday gets its name from the ancient Christian practice of being 'shriven', which means being forgiven for things you've done wrong. It was traditional to tell a priest about anything bad you had done to get it out of the way before Lent, the season of fasting. Then, during the fast, you could concentrate on asking for forgiveness and promising to live a better life. On Shrove Tuesday, people used up eggs and fat because during Lent they were not allowed to eat these things. One of the best ways of using up eggs and fat is to make pancakes, and a lot of people still do this today. That is why we also call this day Pancake Day.

# WEATHER

## "When halo rings moon or Sun, Rain's approaching on the run."

This is an old country saying, and there is some truth in it. If you see a halo around the moon or sun at this time of year, it is because ice crystals can sometimes form in high clouds. These make a ring or 'halo' appear, and later these crystals may fall as rain. Rainy days can seem boring, but remember that the rain is doing a good job of watering all those tiny plants that are waiting for spring to arrive. Also, the rain comes from clouds which come in all shapes and sizes. Cloud spotting can be fun – what kind of pictures and shapes can you see in the clouds today?

## Cloud Spotting

Most of our names for clouds come from Latin. They are a combination of the following:

**Stratus/strato** =
low, flat/layered and smooth

**Cumulus/cumulo =**
heaped up/puffy, like cauliflower

**Cirrus/cirro =**
high up/wispy

**Alto =**
medium level

**Nimbus/nimbo =**
rain-bearing cloud

Combining the names tells you a bit more about the clouds. For example: nimbus + stratus = 'nimbostratus'. This is a cloud which is flat and layered and will probably bring rain. 'Cumulonimbus' is a puffy cloud which will bring rain too.

# SNOW IS FALLING

Christmas cards often have snowy scenes on them, but actually we hardly ever have snow in December in Britain. It is more likely that you will see snow in February. There's nothing like wrapping up warm and running outside to make footprints in the freshly fallen snow.

If you're lucky enough to get lots of snow, you could build a snow castle. Make sure you are wearing warm clothes and waterproof gloves. Make your castle in the same way that you would build a sandcastle – you can pack mounds of snow together with your hands or if you have buckets and spades left over from your summer holiday, you could use them! Make lots of 'turrets' using the buckets or mounds and then join them together with low snow 'walls'. You could make flags with sticks and pieces of paper or strips of old cloth, which you could decorate. Or you could look for stones or interestingly shaped twigs to make patterns on the walls and turrets of your castle.

# WILDLIFE ON THE MOVE

Toads, frogs and newts are often on the move in February. They walk and hop a long way back to their ponds to find others to breed with. This sometimes gets them into trouble, as they have to cross roads between their winter homes and their ponds.

To help prevent the amphibians from getting squashed, there are Toad Patrols up and down the country which go out in the evenings and pick the creatures up and carry them safely across the road. You can help amphibians to migrate safely by joining a patrol near you.

To find a toad crossing near you, go to **www.froglife.org** and follow the links. It's good fun and you can do some stargazing and wildlife watching too, as foxes, badgers and owls are out in the evening as well.

## CAN YOU SPOT...

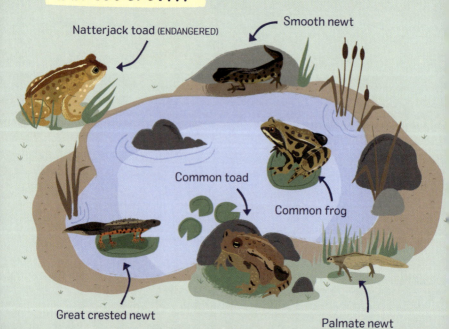

Natterjack toad (ENDANGERED)

Smooth newt

Common toad

Common frog

Great crested newt

Palmate newt

# GREEN FINGERS IN WINTER

There are lots of tidying-up jobs to do outside at this time of year to get the garden ready: so it's all about spring cleaning!

If you have a pond, you need to make sure it doesn't freeze over, as fish won't be able to breathe. You can stop the surface of the pond turning to ice by putting a tennis ball in the water – or even a rubber duck!

You can also get planting for next year. Why not put some snowdrop bulbs in the ground or in pots? Maybe ask your school if you can plant some. Mint grows well in pots too. It is delicious added to cooked peas or boiled new potatoes. Add it to a glass of iced sparkling water for a refreshing drink.

## DID YOU KNOW...

February is a great time to get ahead with clearing away weeds in the garden. Wrap up warm and get outside with gloves and a trowel. Make sure you ask an adult to help you spot the weeds first – you don't want to go digging up a lovely plant by mistake!

# FEED THE BIRDS

Small birds are hungry at this time of year. They need to eat all day to get enough food to keep them going through the winter. You can help by making your own treats for the birds using food scraps from home.

You don't need to spend a lot of money on fancy feeders or a beautiful bird table. You'll need to buy the birdseed and nuts, but if you buy a big sack from a garden centre it is cheaper than buying small quantities, and it will last a long time. You can also use a surprising amount of food that is easy to find at home. Raisins, sultanas, other dried fruit or unsalted nuts go down well with any wild bird.

# Make an *Orange Bird Feeder*

These are very easy and fun to make. And the best thing is, you can make yourself a tasty treat too! Ask an adult to help you cut the oranges in half and then use a juicer or squeezer to make some delicious fresh orange juice. Put it in the fridge and enjoy it as a reward once you have finished making these pretty feeders.

## You will need:

**Shallow oven dish**
**Wooden spoon**
**Empty orange halves**
**Saucepan**
**Birdseeds**
**Raisins**
**Unsalted nuts**
**Unsalted nut butter or dairy butter or lard**

1 *Pour the seeds, fruit and/or nuts into the dish and give them a good stir with the wooden spoon.*

2 *Scoop up a handful of the mixture and press it into the orange halves.*

3 *Ask an adult to help you melt the lard or butter you have chosen to use.*

4 *Pour the melted lard or butter into the orange cups.*

5 *Use the wooden spoon to gently pat the mixture down into the orange cups. Let it solidify.*

6 *Put the feeders on a bird table or windowsill.*

# MARCH

## SPECIAL DAYS

**1st** St David's Day (Wales)

**5th** St Piran's Day (Cornwall)

**7th** Purim (Jewish festival)

**8th** Holi (Hindu festival of colours)

**17th** St Patrick's Day (Ireland)

**19th** Mother's Day

**20th** Spring equinox (first day of spring)/
Ostara (pagan celebration)

**22nd** Ramadan begins (Muslim month of prayer and fasting)

**26th** Daylight saving (clocks go forward)

# ANNIVERSARIES

**90 years ago . . .**

On 2 March 1933, the premiere of the film *King Kong* was shown in New York City.

On 7 March 1933, the first Monopoly board was created by board game inventors in the United States.

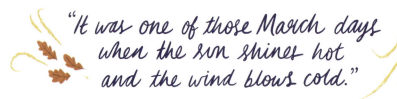

> *"It was one of those March days when the sun shines hot and the wind blows cold."*

CHARLES DICKENS (1812–1870)

This quote describes very well how we might look out of the window in March and think, 'It looks lovely out there!' only to go outside and find ourselves shivering our socks off! At least the days are continuing to get longer. After 26th March this year we will have one extra hour of daylight, when the clocks go forward. There will be many more flowers and baby animals to see, and the birds will be singing their hearts out.

## DID YOU KNOW...

The Anglo-Saxons called March *Hyd* monath which means 'stormy month' or *Hraed* monath which means 'rugged month' because the weather is often so cold and unpredictable at this time of the year.

## *Phases of the Moon* in March 2023

| Full Moon | Last Quarter | New Moon | First Quarter |
|---|---|---|---|
| 7th March | 15th March | 21st March | 29th March |

## Spring Equinox

20th March is the spring equinox. This is one of the days in the year in which the number of hours of daylight is exactly equal to the number of hours of darkness. This happens because the rays of the sun are shining straight at the equator (the middle of the Earth).

## Constellation of the Month

Ursa Major can be seen to the north at this time of year. Its name is Latin for 'Great Bear'. The Romans had a story that a beautiful woman called Callisto was transformed into a bear by the goddess Artemis and thrown up into the stars. The seven brightest stars of this constellation form a saucepan shape often known as the 'Plough' or the 'Big Dipper'.

# FESTIVAL FUN

## 7th March *Purim*

Purim begins on the evening of the 6th and ends on the evening of 7th March. It is a Jewish holiday during which Jewish people remember that long ago their people were saved from Haman, a cruel man who worked for the king of Persia. At Purim, people have a big feast and send money and gifts of food to people in need. It is a time to think of others and be thankful for a good life.

## 8th March *Holi*

Holi is a Hindu festival also known as the 'festival of colours' or the 'festival of love', when Hindus celebrate the victory of good over evil and the arrival of spring. They meet to play and laugh, forget and forgive, and make up with people they have fallen out with! Holi lasts for a night and a day, starting on the evening of the Purnima (full moon day). People light bonfires and pray that evil will be destroyed. Then they smear each other with coloured paints and drench each other using water pistols and water-filled balloons!

## 19th March *Mother's Day*

Mother's Day (or Mothering Sunday) always falls on the fourth Sunday in Lent, three weeks before Easter Day. It was originally a Christian festival, and it has now become a day for people to say thank you to their mothers or carers. Why not make a card or welly-boot planter (p. 43) to show your mother or carer how much they mean to you?

### 20th March  *Ostara*

Ostara is a pagan festival which is celebrated at the spring equinox. For pagans, it's a time of year when everything in the natural world is in perfect balance because the day and the night are the same length. The festival takes its name from Ostara or Ēostre, the goddess of renewal and rebirth, who has the head of a hare.

### 22nd March  *Ramadan Begins*

The month of Ramadan traditionally begins after the new moon, so the date for Ramadan changes from year to year. During Ramadan, Muslims hold a fast during the hours of daylight, which means they are not allowed to eat or drink from the moment the sun comes up until the moment it sets. People must also try not to gossip or fight during Ramadan. Muslims use the daylight hours to focus on saying prayers and giving money and possessions to charity. Some people try to learn the whole holy book, the *Qur'an*, during this time!

## 1st March  *St David's Day*

St David is the patron saint of Wales, and St David's Day is celebrated on 1st March. His name in Welsh is Dewi Sant, and if you want to say Happy Saint David's Day in Welsh you say, *Dydd Gŵyl Dewi Hapus!* He is buried in St David's Cathedral in the city of St David's in Pembrokeshire. People used to travel there in the Middle Ages to pay their respects to him.

There are two plants that are associated with this day – the daffodil and the leek. Leeks used to be worn as a symbol of Welsh pride, but nowadays you are more likely to see people wear a daffodil, which is obviously prettier! But you can't cook a nice pasta dish with daffodils, so here is a recipe for a pasta bake with leeks and bacon for St David's Day. You can substitute the bacon for mushrooms if you prefer.

## Recipe for *St David's Day Pasta*

**You will need:**

**Sharp knife**
**Large non-stick frying pan**
**Large saucepan**
**Wooden spoon**
**Colander**
**Mug or small measuring jug**

**1 tablespoon of olive oil**
**2 tablespoons of water**
**300 g leeks, washed and finely sliced**
**8 rashers of smoked streaky bacon, chopped into squares (One packet of mushrooms for a meat-free option)**
**400 g pasta shapes**
**100 g garlic and herb cream cheese**

1. *Heat the oil in the frying pan on a medium heat on the hob.*
2. *Add the chopped leeks to the pan with the two tablespoons of water.*
3. *Cook for about 10 minutes until the leeks are nice and soft.*
4. *Add the chopped bacon or mushrooms to the leeks and turn up the heat to fry, stirring occasionally with the spoon.*
5. *While the bacon or mushrooms are cooking, cook the pasta shapes in boiling water in the saucepan, following the instructions on the packet.*
6. *Drain the pasta in the colander and keep back about a mug's worth of the cooking water.*
7. *Spoon the cream cheese into the bacon or mushroom and leek mix and add the cooking water from the pasta.*
8. *Mix the drained pasta into the creamy sauce.*

## TOP TIP

If you like your pasta really cheesy, grate over some Parmesan or other hard cheese when you serve it up!

# GET PLANTING!

Now is the perfect time to start planting things. And it's a great idea to plant something that grows pretty quickly because then you don't have to wait too long to see the results. A bean will sprout within one to two weeks. If you take care of it and plant it out carefully, you'll have a whole beanstalk full of delicious beans by the summer. Or why not plant a beautiful springtime flower, such as a daffodil or hyacinth?

## Make a *Welly-boot Planter*

It's not just the plants that are growing fast at this time of year – your feet are growing fast too! This means you might have an old pair of wellies lying around which are too small for you now or which have been so well worn that they have holes in. Don't throw them out! Make them into these fun planters instead. Ask an adult to help with using any sharp tools.

**You will need:**

**Old pair of wellies**
**Pair of scissors or a**
**sharp gardening tool**
**Some soil and compost**
**Trowel**
**Gardening gloves**
**Some bulbs or some**
**pots of spring flowers**
**(daffodils, hyacinths**
**or primroses work well)**

1 *Make a few holes in the bottom of the wellies so that the planters will drain well.*
2 *Fill the boots with soil and compost.*
3 *Plant them with bulbs if you want to wait and watch the flowers grow.*
4 *Or if you can't wait, plant some ready-grown spring flowers!*
5 *Put the boots on your doorstep – they are bound to make your visitors smile.*
6 *Or give them to your mother or female relative or carer for a Mother's Day present!*

43

# OUT AND ABOUT

There are more birds and animals to see in March. Some of them, such as chiffchaffs and wheatears, are visitors from other countries. It will depend where you live in Britain as to whether you are likely to see these birds. Some of them are found only in wetland areas or by the sea.

## CAN YOU SPOT...

Chiffchaff

Sand martin

Sandwich tern

Blackcap

Chaffinch

Wheatear

Skylark

Lapwing

## DID YOU KNOW...

Skylarks start singing before the sun rises, so their voice is one of the first to be heard in the dawn chorus. Sadly, the numbers of skylarks are falling across Western Europe. It is thought that this is because crops are now sown in autumn rather than in spring – this means that skylarks no longer have the habitat they need in which to breed and survive.

# MARCH MADNESS!

Did you know that in March, hares start to behave in a strange way? If you are lucky enough to spot any, you'll probably see them crazily leaping about.

You might even find them standing on their back legs and boxing each other with their paws! This behaviour seems so weird that we sometimes use the expression 'mad as a March hare' to describe a human who is acting in a bizarre way.

Actually, there is a very good reason why hares act like this in March: the male hares are looking for females to mate with at this time of year. The hares box and chase each other as they try to find mates.

# DOWN BY THE RIVER

If you can get to a river, keep a sharp lookout for kingfishers. At this time of year the male bird is very busy, zipping along the surface of the water looking for fish.

## CAN YOU SPOT...

**TOP TIP**
Write down what you find in your nature notebook!

Frog

Frog spawn

Tadpoles

Pond snail

Whirligig beetle

Backswimmer

Pond skater

Dragonfly nymph

Newt

# GET WET

Building a dam is a great outdoors activity now that spring is on its way. You'll need to ask an adult to help you find the best place to build your dam. And make sure everyone wears wellies and some waterproof clothing!

First choose a narrow stream of clean, shallow water where you can paddle safely. Then you need to start looking for driftwood, loose mud, rocks and pebbles. You'll use these to build the dam. You'll find the best bits and pieces at places where the stream bends, as rocks and things tend to get stuck there.

Don't forget to take down your dam before you go home so that the stream can flow freely again.

See if you can stop the stream from flowing or change its direction by building up your dam. Where does the water go?

## DID YOU KNOW...

Beavers create dams to make a pond of deep, quiet water. They use their sharp teeth and strong jaws to bite through the trunks of trees. The trees fall into the water to make a sort of pond. Then the beavers chew off branches and sticks to make islands of wood in the pond in order to build their homes or 'lodges'.

# APRIL

## SPECIAL DAYS

**1st**    April Fool's Day

**5th**    Pesach begins (Jewish celebration)

**9th**    Easter Sunday (Christian celebration)

**22nd**  Earth Day/Eid al-Fitr (end of Ramadan)

**23rd**  St George's Day (England)/William Shakespeare's birthday

# ANNIVERSARIES

### 60 years ago ...

On 30 April 1963, the Bristol Bus Boycott was held. This was a protest against the Bristol Omnibus Company who had refused to let Black or Asian people work on the buses. The protest attracted the attention of the national press and helped to raise awareness about the way Black and Asian people were being unfairly treated in Britain.

### 70 years ago ...

On 13 April 1953, *Casino Royale*, the first James Bond novel written by Ian Fleming, was published.

> *"The sun was warm
> but the wind was chill.
> You know how it is
> with an April Day"*

ROBERT FROST (1874–1963)

The weather can be so confusing in April, as the quote above suggests: you could look out of the window and see bright sunshine, but then when you go outside it might be freezing cold! And then there are those April showers that seem to come without warning, too. Still, without that rain, we wouldn't see the gorgeous blossoms that starts to come out at this time of year.

The mornings are often very cold in April. Sometimes there are still sharp frosts overnight and you might see white feathers of ice crystals on the grass when you wake up. If you live in the hills, you might also get snow.

But then on other days, there will be a bright burst of hot spring weather and you'll feel like running around in a T-shirt and shorts! Basically, the best advice to follow is to be prepared for all weathers – so don't forget to take an umbrella and a jumper out with you this month, even if the sun is shining when you leave the house!

## April Birth Signs

 **Aries** The sign of the ram. This is the sign for people born between 21st March and 19th April and they are supposed to be brave, determined, confident and honest. They can also be impatient, moody and short-tempered – just like a ram, butting his head against things. . .

 **Taurus** The sign of the bull. Some people believe anyone with a birthday that falls between 20th April and 21st May is born under this sign. They are supposed to be sensible and good at making and fixing things.

## DID YOU KNOW...

The birth signs are divided into the four elements of nature: earth, air, fire and water.

*Earth* **Taurus, Virgo, Capricorn**
These signs represent people who are realistic and loyal and who will stick with their family and friends through hard times.

*Air* **Gemini, Libra, Aquarius**
People born under these signs are friendly and communicative and enjoy giving advice.

*Fire* **Aries, Leo and Sagittarius**
People born under these signs might get angry quickly, but they will also forgive easily. They are adventurers who are always ready for action.

*Water* **Cancer, Scorpio and Pisces**
These signs are linked to people who love deep conversations and close friendships.

# FESTIVAL FUN

## 1st April *April Fool's Day*

April Fool's Day is celebrated by people playing tricks on one another. Sometimes there are even April Fool's Day stories on the news. One of the most famous of these was in 1957 on the BBC television programme *Panorama*. The programme reported that in Italy there were spaghetti trees! Lots of people believed this because in 1957 not many people in Britain had eaten spaghetti, so they didn't know that it was made from flour and water and it definitely did not grow on trees . . .

## DID YOU KNOW . . .

April Fool's Day in France is called 'Poisson d'avril' which translates as 'April fish!' People try to stick a paper fish on each other's backs and then shout 'Poisson d'avril!' as a joke!

## 5th April *Pesach*

Jewish people celebrate Pesach to remember how Moses helped the Israelites escape from Egypt to a new life in the Promised Land. They left in such a hurry that the dough from their bread had not risen, so that is why Jewish people eat *matzo* at Pesach today – a flat bread which is 'unleavened'. This means it has no yeast in it and so does not rise like a normal loaf of bread.

The Pesach meal is called the *seder*. During the seder, Jewish families read and tell stories, eat special foods and sing songs, and children ask the adults questions about Pesach.

## Make a *Garden in an Egg Cup*

Spring is the time of year to celebrate new life springing up everywhere! Parks and gardens and window boxes are bursting with colour as flowers and plants pop up out of the soil after the long, dark winter. You might be having a get-together with friends and family over the spring holidays, so why not make some of these mini gardens which will make your windowsills or kitchen table look joyful and 'spring-y'! If you are having a big meal with friends or family you could make a mini garden for each person who is coming and put a card with their name by the garden so that they know where to sit.

Have fun on a walk, seeing what you can spot to use in your mini gardens! Always wear gloves when collecting things like pine cones, and put your finds in a bag to carry them home safely.

**You will need:**

**Egg cups or any small containers**
**Soil or sand**
**Moss**
**Small flowers or herbs**
**Tiny pebbles or gravel**
**Acorns**
**Beechnuts**
**Alder cones**
**Mini pine cones**

1 *Fill your egg cup or container almost to the top with sand or soil.*
2 *If you can find a small amount of moss on the ground you could use that for grass.*
3 *Use pebbles or gravel if you have them to make a tiny path.*
4 *Arrange your cones and flowers to design a lovely garden.*
5 *Place them on the window sill or table to make the perfect springtime decorations!*

# FESTIVAL FUN

**9th April** *Easter Sunday*

The Christian festival of Easter starts on the Thursday before Easter Sunday with a day called 'Maundy Thursday', when Christians believe that Jesus invited his followers to a meal called the 'Last Supper'. Easter ends on Easter Sunday, when Christians believe that Jesus came back from the dead. It is a time for new life and rebirth. Easter eggs are also popular on this day.

Some people believe that the tradition of giving and receiving Easter eggs comes from the pagan festival Ostara, or Ēostre. The Easter Bunny, who is supposed to bring the eggs, is thought to come from the pagan religion, which has the hare as the symbol of new life. Christians use the symbol of the Easter egg to represent rebirth and the resurrection of Jesus.

# EGG-CELLENT ACTIVITIES

Today, a lot of people in Britain give and receive Easter eggs over the Easter weekend, whether or not they celebrate any religious festivals.

## The Hunt is On!

Easter-egg hunts are always exciting. You could ask an adult to hide mini chocolate eggs outside in the garden or in an area of your local park, or even while you are out on a walk. Then see how quickly you can find them – and don't eat too many on the way!

**Make** *Easter in 3D*

These 3D cards look stunning – and they are very simple to make!

**You will need:**

**A4 piece of white card**
**9 A4 pieces of coloured card**
**Glue stick**
**Scissors**

1 *Fold the A4 card in half.*

2 *Cut out nine egg shapes from the coloured card.*

3 *Stick the first egg shape down in the middle of the A4 card.*

4 *Fold the remaining eight egg shapes in half down the centre line.*

5 *Take two of the folded eggs and stick them on to the first egg so that they form 'wings' like a butterfly.*

6 *Stick the next two eggs to the 'wings' in the same way – the egg will start to look like a fan now.*

7 *Keep going until you have used up all of the folded eggs.*

8 *Glue the last two bits of the 'fan' together until the egg is complete.*

9 *Let the glue dry, then fan your egg out – now you have a 3D Easter egg card!*

## 22nd April  *Eid al-Fitr*

Eid al-Fitr is an Islamic festival that is celebrated by Muslims all over the world. It is the day which ends Ramadan and it falls on or near the date of a new moon. During Eid, Muslim people celebrate with delicious food, by praying and by giving money to charity.

### Recipe for *Eid Biscuits*

**You will need:**

Baking tray
Greaseproof paper
Large bowl
Electric hand whisk
Moon and star-shaped
biscuit cutters
Sieve
Wooden spoon
Rolling pin
Small blunt knife
Wire rack

150 g soft butter
100 g caster sugar
1 large egg
250 g plain flour plus a little
for dusting
1 teaspoon of baking powder
A pinch of salt
1 teaspoon of vanilla extract
150 g icing sugar
Silver and gold sprinkles

1 *Preheat the oven to 180°C/160°C fan/gas mark 4 and line a baking tray with greaseproof paper.*

2 *In a large bowl, whisk together the butter and sugar. When the mixture looks light and creamy, add the egg and mix thoroughly.*

3 *Sieve the flour, baking powder and salt and add to the mixture.*

4 *Add the vanilla extract and mix with a wooden spoon until the mixture looks like dough.*

5 *Place the dough on a work surface sprinkled with flour and roll to about 1 cm thickness.*

6 *Use the cutters to cut out moons and stars and place them on to the lined baking tray (you may need more than one tray, or cook them in batches).*

7 *Bake for 8–12 minutes, until the biscuits are lightly golden around the edges.*

8 *Put the biscuits on a wire rack to cool while you make the icing.*

9 *Make the icing following the instructions on the packet.*

10 *Spread the icing on to the biscuits with a small blunt knife and sprinkle on the decorations – silver for the moons and gold for the stars.*

11 *Serve once the icing has set, or put them in a pretty box and give as a gift!*

# BE GREEN FOR EARTH DAY

22nd April is Earth Day. This is a day to focus on what we can do to help the environment and protect our planet. The first Earth Day was in 1970. It was set up by an American politician called Senator Gaylord Nelson because he thought it was important for children to be taught about the environment in school.

Here are some things you could do on Earth Day (and any other day):

★ Walk or cycle to school instead of going by car or bus.

★ Turn off lights when you leave the room.

★ Turn off electrical appliances such as the TV, chargers and computer at the wall when you are not using them.

★ Try not to use a computer, tablet or the TV at all for just one day!

★ Get outside and find a green space to walk or play in – you don't have to have a garden or live in the country to do this. Find a square or a park and take time to look at the trees, plants, birds and insects.

★ If you have space at home, why not do some spring planting?

★ Ask your grown-ups if you can swap to more environmentally friendly cleaning products. Did you know that you can do a lot of cleaning using natural things such as vinegar, water and lemon juice?

★ Remember to take a cloth bag or a 'bag for life' when you go shopping to avoid using a plastic bag.

★ Did you know that meat production uses much more energy than plants? Try eating vegetarian food for one day. There are lots of delicious recipes to try – some are in this book!

★ Take a refillable drinks bottle out with you instead of buying water or juice in plastic bottles.

# IF YOU GO DOWN TO THE WOODS TODAY

Woodland walks are wonderful in April. Not only can you go looking for wild garlic, you are very likely to see bluebells too.

People once believed that fairies used bluebells to trap humans who were out walking in the woods. You shouldn't go walking through the middle of a patch of bluebells anyway, as you may damage the bulbs and stop them flowering again.

A lot of butterflies come out at this time of year too. They will be busy looking for flowers so that they can gather nectar to eat. See how many different kinds of butterfly you can find.

**TOP TIP**
Bluebells are poisonous, so look, don't touch!

CAN YOU SPOT...

Male brimstone

Large white (also called cabbage white)

Green-veined white

Comma

Peacock

Speckled wood

Orange-tip

Holly blue

Small tortoiseshell

# PARK LIFE

There's lots going on in local parks now that the days are longer and lighter. Why not join a parkrun? You don't have to be a fast runner, so you can chat as you run if you like! And there's often a park café nearby where you can go afterwards to have a well-earned snack and drink.

Look at the website **www.parkrun.org.uk** to find out where your nearest junior parkrun is. You will need to ask an adult to help you register online before you join a parkrun.

If running is not for you, take a scooter, skateboard or bike to the park. Or ask an adult if you can volunteer to walk a dog from your local dogs' home if there is one near you. (Or walk your own dog, of course!)

Whatever you choose to do, getting outside and breathing in the spring air will make you smile.

# HOW DOES YOUR GARDEN GROW?

Once the weather warms up, April is a great time to start planting things. You don't need a big garden – in fact, you don't need a garden at all. A lot of flowers, fruits and vegetables can be planted in pots and grown on a windowsill or patio area.

Beetroot

Lettuce

Strawberries

Carrots

Leek

Peas

**Indoors:**

Courgettes

Squash

Tomatoes

Cucumber

Aubergine

### TOP TIP
Don't forget to water your plants once a day.

## Recipe for *Rhubarb Rumble*

This is fun alternative to rhubarb crumble and can be eaten hot or cold like an ice-cream sundae. Make all of the 'rumble' as there will be some left over and you can freeze it – then get it out and defrost it whenever you fancy having it as a topping on other fruit. It works really well with strawberries! The amount of rhubarb in this recipe will easily serve 4-6 people.

**You will need:**

**Sharp knife**
**Saucepan**
**Wooden spoon**
**Large glass bowl**
**4-6 glass dishes or sundae glasses**
**Lined baking sheet**
**Wire rack**

**500 g rhubarb, chopped into 2 cm chunks**
**200 g caster sugar**
**2 tablespoons of water**
**Whipped cream or ice cream or natural yoghurt**

**For the 'rumble'**

**225 g plain flour**
**Pinch of salt**
**200 g chilled butter, cut into cubes**
**150 g demerara sugar**
**100 g porridge oats**

1 *Set the oven to 180°C/160°C fan/gas mark 4.*
2 *Put the rhubarb into a saucepan with the caster sugar and water.*
3 *Cover with a lid and simmer on a very low heat for about 15 minutes, stirring once or twice.*
4 *Put all the rumble ingredients into a large glass bowl and then, using the tips of your fingers, rub the butter into the dry ingredients until you have a mixture like breadcrumbs.*
5 *Squeeze the crumbly mix into clumps and then crumble them on to your lined baking sheet.*
6 *Pop the rumble into the oven and let it cook for about 10 minutes, then take it out and give it a bit of a stir so that it browns all over and let it cook for another 10 minutes while you deal with the rhubarb.*
7 *The rhubarb should have gone soft by now, so spoon some into the bottom of the glass dishes or tall sundae glasses, leaving room for the rest of the dessert.*
8 *Get the rumble out of the oven and let it cool on a wire rack for a few minutes.*
9 *Put a good dollop of whipped cream or ice cream or natural yoghurt on top of the rhubarb.*
10 *Add some rumble, and you're good to go!*

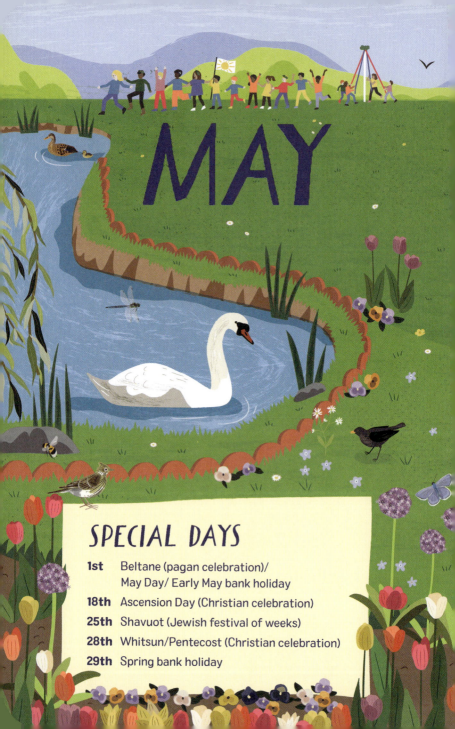

# MAY

## SPECIAL DAYS

**1st**   Beltane (pagan celebration)/
May Day/ Early May bank holiday

**18th**  Ascension Day (Christian celebration)

**25th**  Shavuot (Jewish festival of weeks)

**28th**  Whitsun/Pentecost (Christian celebration)

**29th**  Spring bank holiday

# ANNIVERSARIES

**70 years ago . . .**

On 29 May 1953, the mountaineers Sir Edmund Hillary and Tenzing Norgay were the first people to climb to the top of the world's highest mountain in the Himalayas, named Mount Everest. The historic Tibetan name for it is Chomolungma which means 'Goddess Mother of the World'.

**490 years ago . . .**

On 23 May 1533, King Henry VIII divorced his first wife, Catherine of Aragon. He went on to marry Anne Boleyn.

*"A swarm of bees in May Is worth a load of hay."*

Hedgerows are at their most beautiful in May. They are full of wildflowers which attract lots of insects and butterflies. The traditional saying above gives us a good picture of what is going on in nature in May. It is a very busy month for bees! They are working hard to gather nectar to feed on, and while they do this, they are also helping plants to grow through 'pollination'. So lots of busy bees in May means plenty of yummy fruit and vegetables for us. It's a good idea to plant wildflowers in your garden or allotment if you can, as they will feed the bees.

At the beginning of the month there is also an explosion of golden dandelions and ragwort everywhere. Birds such as goldfinches love the seeds: you'll see lots of these beautiful birds flocking to nibble the seeds just before the flowers turn into dandelion 'clocks'.

## Why is May Called May?

Nobody knows for sure, but it seems likely that this month was named after the Greek goddess Maia, who was goddess of fertility. Her festival is still celebrated by some people on 15th May.

## DID YOU KNOW...

The birthstone for people born in May is the emerald.
It is the stone of love, rebirth and fertility and is
believed to be one of Cleopatra's favourite gemstones.

**Meteor Shower** *Eta Aquariids*

These meteors usually fall sometime between 19th April and
28th May. This year, you should be able to see the shower from
the night of 6th May to the morning of 7th May. About 30
meteors will fall each hour. The shower is formed by
particles of dust left behind by Halley's Comet.
This comet has been known about since
ancient times and can be seen from
Earth without using a telescope.

If you want to see the meteor
shower, you will have to stay
up late or get up very early! The
best spot to see it from is a very
dark place from about midnight.
The meteors can appear
anywhere in the sky.

*Phases of the Moon* **in May 2023**

| **Full Moon** | **Last Quarter** | **New Moon** | **First Quarter** |
|---|---|---|---|
| 5th May | 12th May | 19th May | 27th May |

# FESTIVAL FUN

## 1st May *Beltane*

The old Gaelic word *Beltane* means 'bright fire'. This ancient pagan festival celebrates the return of summer and marks the time of year halfway between the spring equinox and the summer solstice.

Long ago, it was a time when farmers let their cows and sheep back out into the fields after the cold weather. Farmers lit big bonfires with special herbs inside. They would then make their animals walk in between the fires so that they could breathe in the purifying smells. This was supposed to protect them from illness.

## 1st May *May Day*

May Day celebrations are often mixed in with Beltane bonfires. A May queen is chosen and either two people carry her, or she rides through the streets on a cart pulled by a horse. The cart is covered in flowers and the May queen wears flowers in her hair. She sometimes has a man or boy with her representing the Green Man, who is the pagan god of nature. People dance around a maypole, which is a long stick with coloured ribbons coming from the top. Each person takes a ribbon and dances around the pole, weaving in and out of each other until the pole is tightly wrapped in the ribbons.

## 18th May *Ascension Day*

Ascension Day is a Christian festival and a very important date in the Christian calendar. The word 'ascension' means 'rising up'. According to the *Bible*, 40 days after Easter Sunday Jesus ascended, or rose up, to heaven and went to sit at the right-hand side of God. Ascension Day is always celebrated on a Thursday. However, not all countries hold the feast on this day. In Germany, Father's Day is celebrated on the same day.

## DID YOU KNOW...

'Hobby horses' are a May Day tradition. Originally a hobby horse was not just a model horse's head on a stick, like the toys you see today. It was a costume for the May Day parade which made the person wearing it look as though they were riding a real horse.

## 25th May *Shavuot*

Shavuot is a Jewish festival during which Jewish people remember the day that God gave the Prophet Moses the holy scriptures, the *Torah*. Jewish people believe that Moses received the *Torah* from God on a mountain called Mount Sinai in Israel.

Shavuot always comes 50 days after the second day of Pesach. Women and girls light candles to welcome in the holiday, and some Jewish people stay up all night learning the *Torah*.

All Jewish people go to the synagogue on the first day of Shavuot to hear the reading of the Ten Commandments. This is a list of laws for living a good life. They can be found in the *Torah*, the *Qu'ran* and in the *Bible* too.

## 28th May *Pentecost or Whitsun*

Pentecost or Whitsun is the seventh Sunday after Easter. On this day, Christians remember that God sent the Holy Spirit to be with the followers of Jesus. In the north-west of England some churches and chapels still hold 'Whit walks' – parades that include brass bands, choirs and girls dressed in white.

**Make a** *May Day Crown*

This is a fun activity that everyone can get involved in, as you can start by going for a walk and looking for things to add to the crown. Take time to stop and smell the flowers you find. See which ones you recognise when you are on your walk. It doesn't matter if you don't want to wear the crown when it's finished, you could use it as a decoration at home, or give it to a friend or relative to wear – tell them you are crowning them Queen or King of May!

If you see flowers you don't recognise, take a photo of them and look them up when you get home – it is important not to pick a flower you don't know. Remember never to pick endangered flowers such as orchids and bluebells, and never pick flowers that are in private or community gardens, allotments, parks or in nature reserves. Take only petals that have fallen on the ground – do not pull them off flowers that are growing. (You can also use flowers and herbs from a garden if you have asked the gardener for permission first!)

### You will need:

**Grasses**
**Daisies**
**Ragged robin**
**Celandines**
**Red campion**
**Dandelions**
**Buttercups**
**Wild garlic**
**Leaves**
**Petals**
**Feathers**

*Have you ever made a daisy chain? This May crown is very similar. You need to make a slit in the stem of each flower or grass stem with your fingernail, then thread the flower, feather or grass through the hole. Leaves and petals can be threaded on to grass and flower stems.*

*Keep adding flowers and so on until the chain is long enough to fit around the head of the wearer. To join the ends together, make another slit in the last stalk, then push the first flower head through and open out the petals to make a sort of button. This will hold the chain together in a circle.*

*Not only have you made a May Day crown, but you now have a lovely memory of your May Day walk as well!*

# TAKE ME TO THE RIVER

One of the most relaxing things you can do on a sunny day in May is to get out in a boat! There are many places all over Britain where you can hire kayaks, canoes, rowing boats or paddleboards. It is the best way to see river wildlife as you are usually moving slowly and quietly and you are at the same level as many of the animals, birds and insects. If you spot something up ahead, stop paddling and float slowly and quietly towards what you want to observe. It's a good idea to bring binoculars with you.

This is a perfect time of year for spotting brown trout which rise to the surface to eat the hatching mayflies. There will also be lots of little ducklings, cygnets, goslings and chicks around. Moorhen chicks have extremely fluffy black bodies with incredibly long legs and huge feet!

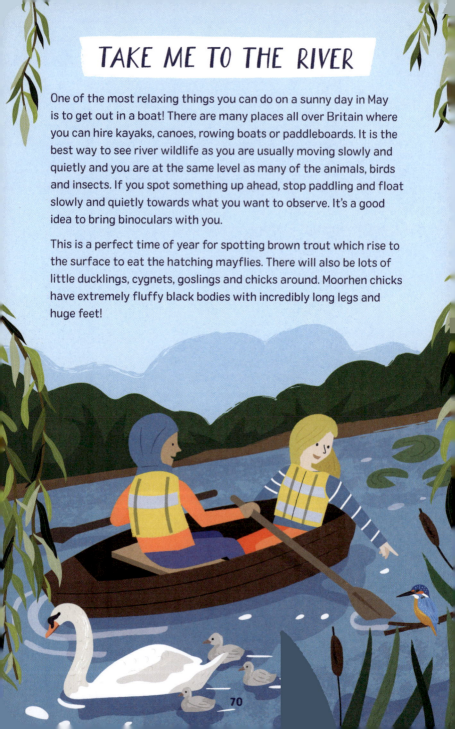

You should also look out for kingfishers which will be hunting a lot at this time of year, catching fish, of course, but also tadpoles.

See if you can see any of these fish, birds or mammals when you are down by the river this month. You might need to take a pair of binoculars with you. Sit very still and be prepared to wait for a while. Wildlife will only appear when it is safe to do so, and if you are noisy you might frighten the creatures away!

CAN YOU SPOT...

Kingfisher

Heron

Canada goose

Mallard female and ducklings

Mute swan and cygnet

Minnow

Tadpoles

# COUNTRYSIDE CODE

Did you know that there are rules you should follow when you are out walking in the countryside? They are designed to make the countryside safe for everyone so that we can all enjoy it.

**1 Respect the local community**

Farmers work hard all year round to grow the food we eat and to look after their animals. If you see a farm animal, remember it is not a pet. Do not feed or stroke it. And if you are in a car or on a bike, make sure you slow down for farm animals so you don't frighten them.

**2 Leave gates as you find them**

If you walk up to a gate and it is closed, make sure you close it behind you. The farmer probably wants to keep the animals from running away. However, if you find a gate open, do not close it behind you as a farmer might be moving animals from one field to the next.

**3 Stick to paths and follow signs**

Some land is open to everyone to walk on, but some is private. If you are not sure, check a detailed map and follow the signs. This is for your own safety as well as to respect people's privacy and to help look after important habitats. You wouldn't want to walk into a field with an old mine shaft, or a pair of ground-nesting lapwings.

#### 4 Leave no trace

Always take your litter away with you. Many places in the countryside do not have public bins but this doesn't mean you can drop your rubbish on the ground. Litter could start a wildfire and is dangerous to wildlife and farm animals as they can hurt themselves on it or end up eating it which could make them seriously ill.

#### 5 Look after your dog

It is important to keep dogs under control in case they run into a field of farm animals and scare them. Look out for signs asking you to keep your dog on the lead. If you have to walk through a field of cows, your dog should be on a lead, but if you are approached by the cows, it would be better to let your dog off their lead. The dog will be safer and so will you. Always remember to pick up any mess your dog makes too, and carry it to the nearest dog bin, as this can make farm animals sick!

73

# BABY WILD ANIMAL SPOTTING

There are so many more animals around in May – many of them are babies. May is the perfect time for spotting young fox cubs or badgers. If you have ever watched *Springwatch* on the BBC, you will have seen how active these animals are, particularly at night.

A simple way to try spotting wildlife at night is to dress in dark clothing and sit very quietly in the garden while the sun goes down. Foxes, badgers, hedgehogs and bats become more active in the early evening. They come out of their homes looking for slugs, worms and insects to eat. Now that the weather is warmer, there is a lot more food around!

## Hedgehogs

These lovely little animals are sadly becoming very rare. There are now fewer than half the number of hedgehogs in the wild as there were in the year 2000. This is possibly because there are fewer hedges for them to live in as so many hedgerows have been replaced with fences. The other problem is traffic. Many hedgehogs are killed on the roads. Some towns have special 'hedgehog crossing' signs to warn drivers to go slowly and look out for the creatures.

If you would like to get a hedgehog sign to put up where you live, visit **www.britishhedgehogs.org.uk**

## TOP TIP

Hedgehogs will drink milk if given to them by humans, but it can actually hurt their tummies! Instead, why not leave out a shallow saucer of water for them to enjoy?

## Badgers

You would think it would be easy to spot a badger as their grey bodies and black and white striped faces are very clearly recognisable. However, badgers are nocturnal which means that they tend to sleep in the day and come out at night, and as the evenings are very light in May, you might have to ask if you can stay up late to see if you can spot one!

**DID YOU KNOW...**

Badgers can live up to eight years and weigh as much as 12 kg. They can measure as much as a metre in length.

Badgers are omnivores – in other words, they eat fruit and plants and berries, but they also eat small animals such as mice and voles, as well as birds' eggs and even insects, worms and slugs! You can often tell where a badger has been as they dig up the grass with their long snouts and strong front paws to look for tasty snacks, and sometimes they can make a bit of a mess doing this. Badgers live in family groups in large, underground homes called 'setts'. They keep their living space separate from their toilet space. Their cubs are born in January and February, but the cubs don't come above ground until around now when the weather is warmer and there is more food to find.

# JUNE

## SPECIAL DAYS

**5th**  World Environment Day

**10th**  The Queen's official birthday/
Trooping the Colour (the Queen's
birthday parade)

**18th**  Father's Day

**21st**  Summer solstice

**22nd**  Windrush Day

**24th**  Midsummer's Day

**28th**  Eid al-Adha

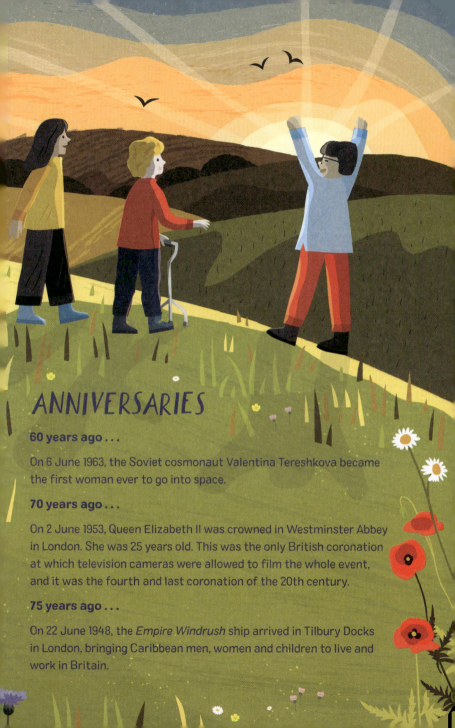

# ANNIVERSARIES

**60 years ago . . .**

On 6 June 1963, the Soviet cosmonaut Valentina Tereshkova became the first woman ever to go into space.

**70 years ago . . .**

On 2 June 1953, Queen Elizabeth II was crowned in Westminster Abbey in London. She was 25 years old. This was the only British coronation at which television cameras were allowed to film the whole event, and it was the fourth and last coronation of the 20th century.

**75 years ago . . .**

On 22 June 1948, the *Empire Windrush* ship arrived in Tilbury Docks in London, bringing Caribbean men, women and children to live and work in Britain.

> *"At midnight, in the month of June,*
> *I stand beneath the mystic moon."*

EDGAR ALLAN POE (1809–1849)

Summertime is here at last! It's time for strawberries and cream and barbecues. The roses are out in the gardens and parks and, of course, there are lots of hot, sunny days to look forward to – right?

Well . . . there will be some sunshine, but often we get excited and plan summer outdoor activities in Britain, only to find that the rain means we have to change our plans.

Nevertheless, this is the month to enjoy long days outside. When you get home from school it feels as though you have so much extra time to have fun! You can meet your friends in the park or just laze around in the shade eating ice cream. June has the longest day of the year, so by 21st June you won't see the sun go down until around 10 p.m. The full moon occurs on 14th June this year, so you'll have to stay up late if you want to see it!

## DID YOU KNOW...

June has both the longest and the shortest days of the year, depending on where you are in the world! If you live in the northern hemisphere, 21st June is the longest day of the year, but if you're in the southern hemisphere, it's the shortest.

## Why is June Called June?

The month of June was probably named after the Roman god Juno. She was the wife of Jupiter, who was the king of the gods. Juno was the goddess of marriage. Some people think it is good luck to get married in June. The Anglo-Saxons called it *Sera monath*, which means 'dry month'. (Maybe it didn't rain so much back then!)

## June Birth Signs

 **Gemini**  The sign of the twins. Anyone born between 21st May and 21st June is a Gemini. They are supposed to be very chatty!

 **Cancer**  The sign of the crab. If your birthday is between 22nd June and 22nd July it is said that you are a Cancer. Cancerians are believed to be shy, sensitive, loving and thoughtful.

## Constellation of the Month

Cassiopeia was a vain queen in Greek mythology. The legend tells us that she was thrown into the sky as a constellation after enraging Poseidon, the god of the sea. She boasted to him that her daughter Andromeda was more beautiful than his sea nymphs. She should have known that it is never a good idea to make an ancient god angry!

### Birthstone and Birth Flower

If your birthday is in June, your birthstone can be either pearl or moonstone. Both are supposed to bring health and long life. The official flower of June is the honeysuckle. Bees, butterflies and birds love this sweet-smelling plant.

# FESTIVAL FUN

**5th June** *World Environment Day*

World Environment Day was set up in 1974 to encourage all of us, including governments and businesses, to look after our planet. Countries take it in turns to host and choose a theme for World Environment Day. For example, when Colombia was the host country, the theme was 'Time for Nature'. The focus was on 'biodiversity' which means the number and variety of all the living things on Earth. Colombia has a very high biodiversity, but because the Amazon rainforest is becoming smaller, the country wanted to raise awareness of the need to protect all life by stopping humans from chopping down the trees in the forest and damaging the natural habitat of everything that lives there.

## TOP TIP
Plant wildflowers such as oxeye daisies and foxgloves in your garden to encourage the bees to come!

## 10th June *The Queen's Official Birthday*

This is always celebrated on the second Saturday in June. The Queen appears on the balcony of Buckingham Palace in London to watch the Trooping of the Colour. The soldiers wear special uniforms to show which regiment they belong to. Music is played by the Foot Guards' Band and the Band of the Household Cavalry, who are on horseback. There are 400 musicians in total!

The Queen gives awards called 'Birthday Honours' to people who have done something special in their lives, such as helping people in their community or charity work.

## 18th June *Father's Day*

Father's Day is a day to remember dads, and also grandfathers or other male relatives or carers who are special people in our lives. You could plan a camping trip with your relative or carer for the night. You don't have to go anywhere special – you could just camp in the garden. Or if it's raining, choose your favourite film to watch together.

81

# 21ST JUNE SUMMER SOLSTICE

*" In winter I get up at night*
*and dress by yellow candle-light.*
*In summer, quite the other way,*
*I have to go to bed by day."*

ROBERT LOUIS STEVENSON (1850–1894)

It can be very annoying when you have to go to bed when the sun is still up! It is particularly hard to go to sleep on the longest day of the year. Pagans traditionally do not go to bed at all on this night! They stay up to welcome the sunrise and give thanks for its power and warmth.

One famous pagan summer solstice celebration happens at Stonehenge, a circle of standing stones in Salisbury in the west of England. People meet at the stones to watch the sunrise at about 4.45 a.m. This is an act of worship and there is a lot of music and dancing.

The summer solstice is also known as *Litha*, which is an Anglo-Saxon word for 'midsummer'. Bonfires were lit on the tops of hills – some places in Britain still do this. The bonfire represents the strength, light and heat of the sun. Young men used to leap over them for luck!

# WINDRUSH DAY

Windrush Day is on 22nd June. On this day in 1948, 1,027 people finally arrived in Britain after making the long journey, thousands of kilometres across the Atlantic from the Caribbean on a ship called the *Empire Windrush*. They came because the British government had advertised jobs for them in Britain.

Lots of young men and women from the Caribbean had served in the British army, navy and air force during the Second World War. When the war ended, they were keen to come to Britain to help rebuild the cities after bombs had destroyed so much of the country. This was the first time so many people had come to Britain from the Caribbean, and many more came in the years that followed, to live with their families and to work here.

## 9th July *Eid al-Adha*

This is an Islamic festival that marks the end of the *hajj* pilgrimage to the holy city of Mecca. It commemorates how Ibrahim was willing to sacrifice his son Isma'il to God. Allah stopped the sacrifice and gave Ibrahim a lamb to kill instead. A version of this story is also found in the Jewish *Torah* and the Old Testament of the Christian *Bible*.

Many Muslims wear new clothes or their nicest outfits for this festival and attend a prayer service at a mosque. They also send Eid cards to family and friends, donate money to charity and give each other gifts.

## Recipe for *Spicy Naan*

Naan – a type of flatbread – is always a good accompaniment to tasty, spicy food, and homemade ones taste so good. This is a delicious and easy recipe, although you have to leave time to allow the dough to rise or 'prove', so read through the recipe before you get started. If you can't find ghee in the shops, you can make it.

**You will need:**

**Large mixing bowl**
**Tea towel or food covering of some kind**
**Rolling pin**
**Baking tray**
**Small bowl**
**Pastry brush**

### For the dough

**450 g strong white bread flour**
**1 teaspoon of salt**
**7 g sachet of dried yeast**
**5 tablespoons full-fat natural yoghurt**
**1 tablespoon ghee, melted**
**200 ml lukewarm tap water**

### For the topping

**5 teaspoons of ghee, melted**
**½ teaspoon of cayenne pepper**
**1 teaspoon of ground coriander**
**1 teaspoon of ground cumin**
**1 teaspoon of garam masala**
**Fresh coriander**

1. *Put the flour, salt and yeast into the mixing bowl.*
2. *Add the yoghurt and the melted ghee.*
3. *Knead the ingredients together with clean hands.*
4. *Gradually add the water until you have a soft dough. It should not become too sticky, so you might not need all the water.*
5. *Tip the dough out on to a floured work surface and knead for 4-5 minutes.*
6. *Return the dough to the mixing bowl and cover it with a cloth or a reusable food covering and leave to rise or 'prove' for one hour. It should double in size.*
7. *Preheat the oven to 180°C/160°C fan/gas mark 4.*
8. *Tip the dough out again and roll it with the rolling pin into a flat pear shape.*
9. *Make the spicy topping by mixing melted ghee with the spices in the small bowl.*
10. *Place the naan dough on the baking tray and bake for 10-12 minutes until it has started to puff up and turn golden brown.*
11. *Remove the naan and brush over half of the spicy topping.*
12. *Place the naan back in the oven and cook for a final 3 minutes.*
13. *Remove the naan and brush over the topping again.*
14. *Serve warm with your favourite curry, stew or soup. Delicious!*

# NAME THAT MINIBEAST!

If you can get to a canal, river, lake or pond, this is a great way to spend a summer afternoon, whatever the weather. In fact, minibeasts are sometimes easier to find on a rainy day, so if it's a typical wet and windy British summer day, just wrap up in your waterproofs, pull on a pair of wellies and get outside for some minibeast fun!

**You will need:**

Fishing net
Bucket
Magnifying glass (optional)
This book!

### TOP TIP
You'll need an adult to help you with this activity if you are near deep water.

First of all, you need to fill your bucket with some water from the river, canal, lake or pond that you are visiting. Then put your net into the river and drag it back and forth gently. Once you have picked up a few minibeasts, tip them quickly and carefully into your bucket.

Now follow this guide to see what you might have found:

**Has it got a shell? It might be:**

Nerite snail

Ramshorn snail

Bivalve mollusc

Wandering pond snail

**Has it got six legs and no tail? It might be:**

Whirligig beetle

Great diving beetle

Lesser water boatman

**Has it got six legs and one tail? It might be:**

**Has it got six legs and two tails? It might be:**

Water stick insect

Water scorpion

Stonefly nymph

Dragonfly nymph

**Is it long and thin? It might be:**

**You might even catch a small fish!**

Riverworm

Hairworm

Stickleback

Minnow

Leech

Flatworm

Bullhead

Lamprey

Bloodworm
(midge larva)

Stone loach

## TOP TIP
Remember to wash your hands after you have finished this activity!

# SUPER STRAWBERRIES

June is the month to enjoy strawberries as they are in season now and at their most juicy and delicious. There are so many things you can do with strawberries, but the best way to eat them in the summer is when they are fresh. Add them to fruit salads or sprinkle them on tarts or ice cream. Or make a quick compote with them to put on top of warm homemade scones with a dollop of clotted cream.

## Recipe for *Scones with Strawberry Compote*

**You will need:**

**Baking tray**
**Sieve**
**Mixing bowl**
**Rolling pin**
**Round, 5 cm pastry cutter**
**Pastry brush**
**Small saucepan**

**For the scones**

225 g self-raising flour
1 tsp baking powder
Pinch of salt
25 g caster sugar
50 g softened, unsalted butter
150 ml full-fat milk
1 free-range egg, beaten

**For the strawberry compote**

250 g strawberries
(plus extra to serve, if you like)
100 g caster sugar
60 ml water

1. *Preheat the oven to 220°C/200°C fan/gas mark 7.*
2. *Lightly grease the baking tray.*
3. *Sieve together the flour, baking powder and salt into the mixing bowl.*
4. *Stir in the sugar and add the butter.*
5. *Using just the tips of your fingers, lightly rub the butter into the dry ingredients until the mixture looks like fine breadcrumbs.*
6. *Add the milk, a little at a time, and stir it into the dry ingredients with your hands to form a smooth dough.*
7. *It is a good idea to let the dough rest for 5-15 minutes before rolling it out if you have time as this helps to make the scones light and fluffy.*
8. *Use the rolling pin to roll out the dough on a lightly floured work surface until it is about 2 cm thick.*
9. *Use the pastry cutter, cut the dough, using one sharp tap. Try not to twist the dough as you cut because this will make the scones go lumpy and bumpy!*
10. *Brush the top of each scone lightly with the beaten egg for a shiny glaze.*
11. *Place them on the baking tray and bake for 10-12 minutes until they have turned golden brown.*
12. *Make the strawberry compote while the scones are baking.*
13. *Take the leaves off the strawberries and cut them in half.*
14. *Place the strawberries in a small saucepan with the sugar and water and simmer for 5 minutes.*
15. *Remove from the heat and set aside to cool and thicken.*
16. *Remove the scones from the oven and let them cool, then cut them in half and add clotted cream and compote to serve with a sprinkling of fresh strawberries on top. Yum!*

## DID YOU KNOW...

In Devon people prefer to spread the clotted cream on before the jam, whereas in Cornwall it is always 'jam first'. You can get into quite an argument about this in the West Country!

# JULY

## SPECIAL DAYS

**9th**     Sea Sunday (Christian celebration)

**12th**    Battle of the Boyne (Northern Ireland)

**15th**    St Swithun's Day

**19th**    Muharram (Islamic New Year)

**25th**    St James's Day (Grotto Day)

# ANNIVERSARIES

**75 years ago . . .**

On 4 July 1948, at midnight, the NHS (National Health Service) was started. This is the service which everybody in Britain can use if they become sick or hurt and need to see a doctor or go to hospital. It was the first health service in the world to be 'free at point of use', which means that anyone could see a doctor without having to pay a doctor's bill. The service is paid for by taxes that adults pay to the government. During the Covid pandemic, people used to go out into the streets to clap and cheer for all the doctors and nurses and carers who worked for the NHS during that time. People also put rainbows and blue hearts in the windows of their homes to say 'Thank you, NHS'.

**100 years ago . . .**

On 13 July 1923, a scientist called George Olsen found some fossil eggs while on an expedition to Mongolia in Central Asia. At first these were thought to be Protoceratops eggs but in fact they were Oviraptor eggs.

## "In scorched July
## The storm-clouds fly."

CHRISTINA ROSSETTI (1830–1894)

At last the school holidays are here – weeks and weeks of free time to do whatever you like! It would be wonderful if we could rely on the weather to be fine for the whole of the holidays, but July can be a particularly stormy month. In fact, you are more likely to experience a thunderstorm during this month than at any other time during the year. This is because storms develop when there is a layer of warm air near the ground underneath a layer of much colder air. This is much more common in the summer when the days are longer, as there is more sunshine and therefore more energy.

But don't worry – there will still be golden days when you can rush to the beach or have long, lazy picnics in the park. And when the weather does break, just pull on some waterproof clothes and go out to splash in the puddles and breathe in the lovely smell of summer rain!

## Why is July Called July?

It was named to honour the Roman statesman
Julius Caesar as it was the month in which he
was born (12th July). Before that, it was known
as *Quintilis* – Latin for 'fifth' – as this was the
fifth month in the Roman year before the
calendar was changed. The Anglo-Saxons
called it *Heymonath* as this is haymaking time.

*Phases of the Moon* **in July 2023**

| **Full Moon** | **Last Quarter** | **New Moon** | **First Quarter** |
|:---:|:---:|:---:|:---:|
| 3rd July | 10th July | 17th July | 25th July |

## Constellation of the Month

Scorpius is Latin for 'scorpion' and is associated with the eighth
sign of the zodiac. It is one of the oldest constellations to be named.
It was officially first recorded in the second century CE by the
Greek mathematician Ptolemy, but 5000 years ago the Sumerians in
the Middle East were already calling this constellation 'the scorpion'
because of its shape. It is quite easy to find because it is near
the middle of the Milky Way. It contains many very bright stars,
including Antares which looks slightly red. In Greek mythology,
Scorpius is linked to Orion the hunter.

### 9th July *Sea Sunday*

Sea Sunday is usually held on the second Sunday in July. It is a Christian festival mainly celebrated by people who live by the sea. On this day, people go to church to say prayers and give thanks for their friends and family members who go out in all weathers to work at sea. Charities and organisations such as the Sailors' Society and the Sea Cadets hold parades and fundraising events.

### 15th July *St Swithun's Day*

On St Swithun's Day there is a saying:

*" St Swithun's Day, if thou dost rain,
for forty days it will remain.
St Swithun's Day, if thou be fair,
for forty days 'twill rain nae mair."*

Thankfully, this is rarely true! St Swithun was the bishop of Winchester. When he died in 862 CE, he was buried in front of the west door of the old Saxon cathedral building because he had said he wanted to be buried outdoors. He lay there for over 100 years. When another bishop came along in 971 CE, he wanted to have a new patron saint, so he dug up poor old St Swithun on his feast day, 15th July, and moved him to a tomb inside! That day there was a terrible storm which lasted for 40 days and 40 nights. Many people believed that this happened because the saint was not happy about being moved indoors, so that is where the saying about the weather comes from.

**19th July** *Muharram*

Muharram is the first month in the Islamic calendar, so this is the time that Muslims celebrate New Year. The Islamic calendar is a lunar calendar which means it follows the phases of the moon and lasts for 354 days, so the date for Muharram is different when compared with the western or 'Gregorian' calendar which is 365 days. In the holy book called the *Hadith* it is written that Musa (sometimes known as Moses) was victorious over the Egyptians on the 10th day of Muharram, so this month is considered a very holy month. Many Muslims fast and pray during Muharram, just as they do in the holy month of Ramadan.

**25th July** *St James's Day or Grotto Day*

There is an old tradition that on St James's Day, children would make 'grottoes' or little caves out of seashells. This is because the scallop shell is supposed to be the symbol for St James, who was one of the followers of Jesus.

Whitstable Oyster Festival begins on St James's Day. An old Kentish tradition says that Julius Caesar went to Britain because he loved the Whitstable oysters! The festival is a celebration of thanksgiving that still survives today.

## Make a *Seashell Grotto*

If you go to the seaside this month, you'll be sure to collect some shells from the beach. Why not make your own St James's grotto by the sea? Make a sandcastle and then decorate it with as many different kinds of shells and pebbles as you can find.

# SEASIDE COLLECTOR'S GUIDE

Wentletrap

Baltic telin

Grey top shell

Oyster

Otter shell

Cockle

Great scallop

Common periwinkle

Flat periwinkle

Common piddock

Common mussel

Spotted cowrie

**Recipe for** *Celebration Biryani*

This is a popular meal for some Muslims when they are breaking a fast. There are lots of different versions of biryani. It is believed that this dish gets its name from the Persian language. *Birinj* means rice and also *birian* means 'fried', so 'biryani' is any dish that has fried food and rice mixed together.

Here is a vegetarian option you might like to try, but you can use beef or chicken or lamb instead of the cauliflower and sweet potatoes. Serve with your favourite chutneys, poppadoms and maybe some of the naan from the recipe in June!

**You will need:**

**Large roasting tin**
**Measuring jug**
**Wooden spoon**
**Kitchen foil**

**2 tablespoons of vegetable oil**
**1 cauliflower, broken into small florets**
**2 sweet potatoes, peeled and cubed**
**1 onion, sliced**
**1 litre vegetable stock**
**3 tablespoons of curry paste**
**1 teaspoon chilli flakes**
**Large pinch of saffron strands**
**500 g basmati rice**
**140 g trimmed green beans**
**Juice of 2 lemons**
**Handful of fresh coriander leaves**
**50 g packet salted roasted cashew nuts (optional)**

1. *Preheat the oven to 220°C/200°C fan/ gas mark 7.*
2. *Ask an adult to help you pour the oil into the roasting tin and put it in the oven for a couple of minutes to heat through.*
3. *Put all the vegetables except the beans in the tin and stir to coat them in the hot oil.*
4. *Add some salt and pepper and return the tin to the oven for 15 minutes until the vegetables begin to brown.*
5. *While the vegetables are roasting, mix the stock, curry paste, chilli and saffron together in a measuring jug.*
6. *Take the roasting tin out and tip in the rice and the green beans, then pour over the stock and cover the dish tightly with foil.*
7. *Lower the oven to 190°C/170°C fan/ gas mark 5.*
8. *Put the tin back in the oven and bake for a further 30 minutes until the rice is tender and the liquid has been soaked up by the rice.*
9. *Stir in the lemon juice and scatter over the coriander and cashew nuts too, if you like.*
10. *Serve with all the extras you want, and enjoy!*

## Build a *Bug Hotel*

Insects and spiders are gardeners' friends! Encouraging small creatures such as bees, beetles and woodlice into your garden at home or school will help the plants to grow – so you'll be doing everyone a favour if you build a lovely shelter for the minibeasts outside.

### You will need:

**Bricks with holes in**
**Wood**
**Old logs**
**Straw**
**Moss**
**Dry leaves**
**Woodchips**
**Old terracotta plant pots**
**Old roof tiles**
**Bark**
**Pine cones**
**Sand**
**Soil**
**Hollow bamboo canes**
**Dead hollow stems from plants**
**Roofing felt**

1. *Choose the spot where you want your hotel to be. Damp places are best for most bugs, but if you want to attract bees you'll need a sunnier spot.*

2. *Put some bricks on the ground to make a strong base, leaving some gaps between them – an H-shape is best.*

3. *Lay planks of wood across the bricks to make a 'floor'.*

4. *Cover the planks with dead wood and bark – beetles, centipedes and woodlice will love this. Spiders too!*

5. *Put some more bricks or blocks of wood on the edges of the 'floor' to add another level.*

6. *Pack this next level with bamboo or other hollow stems for insects to crawl into.*

7. *Keep adding layers filled with other materials until you have the kind of hotel you want.*

8. *To add a roof, you can nail roofing felt on to the last area of wood – ask an adult to help.*

**TOP TIP**

Larger holes
made from broken
flowerpots or tiles are
wonderful homes for
toads and frogs.

# BUSY, BUZZY BEES!

There are more types of bee than you probably realise! Here are some of the ones you'll see in Britain.

Honeybee

Garden bumblebee

Patchwork leafcutter bee

Red mason bee

Red-tailed bumblebee

Common carder bee

Tree bumblebee

Honeybees are extremely important pollinators for flowers, fruits and vegetables. This means that they help other plants grow! Bees transfer pollen between the male and female parts of a plant, and plants can then grow seeds and fruit.

### Top Five Bee Facts

★ There are more than 25,000 different species of bee in the world!

★ Male honeybees in the hive are called drones and they do not have a stinger.

★ Worker honeybees are females. They do all the different tasks needed to operate and maintain the hive.

★ An average beehive can hold around 50,000 honeybees.

★ The queen bee lays all of the eggs in a colony. At the height of the season, she may lay over 2,500 eggs per day!

# MAGICAL MOTHS

Some people find moths annoying, but they are extremely beautiful and it is worth observing them up close to see the intricate patterns on their wings. Use this spotter's guide to help you identify some.

## CAN YOU SPOT...

### Large yellow underwing

*This moth has narrow, rounded top wings. They are either a reddish or blackish brown with a mottled pattern. The wings underneath are orange and have a black band along the edge.*

### Burnished brass

*This moth is a gorgeous mix of orange, brown and gold, with panels of metallic greenish yellow.*

### Setaceous Hebrew character

*This is a very common moth. Look for the striking pale triangle which sits on either side of the wings.*

### Ruby tiger

*This moth is bright red and has a cute furry head. Its 'woolly bear' caterpillars are a favourite food of the cuckoo.*

### Garden tiger

*This moth has stunning spots and patterns on its wings. It squeaks at bats to let them know that it's poisonous!*

### Angle shades

*This moth is often mistaken for a dead leaf!*

### Green carpet

*This pretty moth has a green and black marbled pattern on its wings. As the moth gets older, the green fades to a yellowish or pinkish white.*

### Antler moth

*This moth has a distinctive lightning-strike shape that branches off down either wing. You might even see this one during the day.*

# BE A FOSSIL DETECTIVE

One hundred years ago, a man called Roy Chapman Andrews returned from the Gobi Desert with the news that his team of scientists had discovered the first dinosaur eggs. Newspapers around the world were so excited – they all wanted to be the first to report on this fantastic fossil find. In fact, the discovery had been made years before, but the men who had found the eggs didn't realise exactly what they were!

Did you know that you can be a modern-day fossil detective? There are remains of ancient living creatures and plants preserved in rock up and down the country. People find them in all shapes and sizes, from the smallest seashell to the hugest dinosaur skeleton! Fossils are very rare and they can be difficult to find, but you might be lucky.

## DID YOU KNOW...

The most ancient fossils that have been found so far are around 3.45 million years old!

## How Are Fossils Formed?

It takes millions of years for fossils to form. Sometimes small creatures are fossilised in something called 'amber' which is the sap or resin from plants and trees that has become hard over time. Some fossils are made from bone or wood that has turned into stone, and some are made from animals and plants that fell quickly right to the bottom of rivers and were buried deep in the mud or sand.

There are many different kinds of fossil. If you do go fossil hunting, remember to follow the Fossil Code:

1 **Take a grown-up with you.**

2 **Stay away from cliffs and cliff edges.**

3 **Check the tides and the weather before you go – only ever hunt for fossils when the tide is going out and never go in bad weather.**

4 **Only collect things that have come out of the ground naturally or have been washed up by the sea.**

# FOSSIL GUIDE

Gryphea

Ammonite

Shark tooth

Belemnite

Sea sponge

Sea urchin

## TOP TIP
If you find a fossil, see if you can trace its shape on to paper with a pencil or make a rubbing with crayons.

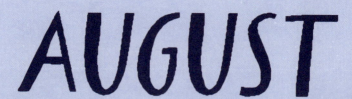

# AUGUST

## SPECIAL DAYS

**1st**    Lammas/Lughnasadh (pagan celebrations)

**7th**    Summer bank holiday (Scotland)

**27th**    Notting Hill Carnival

**28th**    Summer bank holiday (England, Northern Ireland and Wales)

**30th**    Raksha Bandhan (Hindu celebration)

# ANNIVERSARIES

**60 years ago . . .**

On 28 August 1963, Martin Luther King Junior gave a famous speech in Washington DC in the USA, which started, "I have a dream". He made a powerful argument for all people to be treated equal, no matter what the colour of their skin.

**2,053 years ago . . .**

In August 30 BCE, Cleopatra, Queen of Ancient Egypt and one of the most famous women rulers in ancient history, died at the age of 39. She began her rule alongside her father and brothers, but ended ruling on her own. There are many stories and works of art that celebrate her life, including Shakespeare's play, *Antony and Cleopatra*. Some stories say that she bathed in donkey's milk every day to keep her skin soft!

*"In August when the days are hot,
I like to find a shady spot."*

In August, it can feel as though the summer holidays will stretch on forever. You can enjoy the long, sunny days and spend as much time outside as possible. Perhaps you will be lucky enough to go to another country for your holiday, but if not there is more than enough to do closer to home. Days by the seaside or down by the river or playing in the parks or woods near your home offer lots of opportunities for activities and fun things to do with your friends and family.

Or perhaps you are the sort of person who likes to do nothing at all on a sunny day? Sometimes it's lovely just to find a spot of shade where you can read or snooze or sit and watch the world go by. Whatever you choose to do this August, make the most of all your free time and enjoy yourself!

### Why is August Called August?

The Roman Emperor Augustus Caesar thought that since there was a month named after his great-uncle Julius there should be one named after him too! So *Sextilis* or the 'sixth month', was changed to August in the year 8 BCE in his honour. The Anglo-Saxons called it *Weodmonath*, which means 'weed month' as so many weeds grow at this time of year.

### Birth Flower and Birthstone

The flower for this month is the poppy, which represents strength, love, marriage and family. The stone is called peridot. It is an unusual olive-green colour and contains a lot of iron. Peridot is formed in the magma of volcanoes and comes to the surface when volcanoes erupt.

## August Birth Signs

**Leo** The sign of the lion. Some people believe that anyone with a birthday which falls between 23rd July and 22nd August is born under this sign. They are said to be enthusiastic, passionate and generous.

**Virgo** The sign of the maiden. It is said that people with a birthday between 23rd August and 22nd September are born under this sign. Virgos are thought to be good friends, kind and sensitive.

## Planet Spotting

Mercury is at its highest point above the sun in the evening sky in the first half of this month. If you want to try and spot it, look out towards the west as the sun is setting. It will be hanging low in the sky, just above the horizon.

Saturn will be at its closest to the Earth towards the end of the month. The sun will be shining right on Saturn at this point in the year so it will be at its brightest. You should be able to see it at any point during the night, as long as the sky is clear. If you have a telescope you will be able to spot Saturn's rings and a few of its moons.

# FESTIVAL FUN

**1st August** *Lammas*

Lammas is a pagan celebration of the first harvest, and is a time for giving thanks. The word *lammas* comes from the phrase 'loaf mass' which is a special celebration of the first grain to be cut in the harvest, and the first loaf to be made from that grain.

Lammas is also the name of the grain goddess, harvest queen and Earth mother. The harvest god is called John Barleycorn.

## DID YOU KNOW…

In the old days, once the last sheaf of grain of the harvest had been cut, the sheaf was made into a 'corn dolly' and carried through the village. If the harvest was good, the dolly was made into a pretty 'corn maiden' and if it was bad, it was made into an ugly 'corn hag'. How rude!

**1st August** *Lughnasadh*

On this day there is also an old Celtic festival called Lughnasadh – the festival of Lugh or Lug, the Celtic sun king and god of light. The celebrations include feasting, market fairs, games, bonfire celebrations and circle dancing. This is a time to remember that the power and energy of Lugh (the sun) is now slowing down and the darker days of winter are just around the corner.

### 30th August  *Raksha Bandhan*

This is a Hindu festival celebrated at the full moon. The name *Raksha Bandhan* means the 'bond of protection'. *Raksha* means 'protection' and *bandhan* means 'to tie'. The festival celebrates the relationship between brothers and sisters. During the festival, sisters tie a *rakhi* (holy thread) around their brothers' wrists as a symbol to show that they are praying for their brothers' protection and care. The brothers in return vow to look after their sisters, and give them a present.

The best time to tie rakhi on Raksha Bandhan is during *aparahna*, which is late afternoon.

# FIRE, FIRE, BURNING BRIGHT

The Celtic festival of Lughnasadh is a festival of light which includes bonfires and feasting. Why not make the most of the last days of summer by having a barbecue on your patio or in the garden? August might be the last chance for you to do this before the autumn sets in! Remember to ask an adult to help.

If you don't have a garden or patio big enough to do this, you can still enjoy the feasting part of Lughnasadh! Have a go at making these delicious veggie burgers indoors instead, then wrap them in foil and take them to the park or beach and enjoy them on one of those lovely long summer evenings. Remember to take any litter home with you so that you 'leave no trace' – the wildlife and plants will thank you for it!

## Recipe for *Tasty Halloumi Burgers*

**You will need:**

**Barbecue and charcoal (optional)**
**Pastry brush**
**Tongs**

**250 g halloumi cheese, cut into 8 slices**
**1 tablespoon of olive oil**
**4 burger buns, split open**
**4 tablespoons of hummus**
**1 or 2 large tomatoes, sliced**
**Crunchy lettuce such as iceberg or little gem**
**Ketchup or any other sauces you like!**

**1** *If using a barbecue, ask an adult to help you lay the charcoal and light it. You'll need to leave the charcoal to go white before you start cooking.*

**2** *Brush both sides of all the slices of halloumi with the olive oil.*

**3** *Barbecue or grill the cheese on both sides until it is just golden brown. Do not overcook.*

**4** *This should take only 2 or 3 minutes each side. Use the tongs to turn the cheese.*

**5** *Toast the burger buns if you like, but again, only for 2 or 3 minutes.*

**6** *Spread hummus on one half and any other sauce you fancy on the other half: ketchup, mayonnaise, chilli sauce, brown sauce – your choice!*

**7** *Add a couple of slices of halloumi, tomato and lettuce. You can add other toppings too. Avocado also goes well with this.*

**8** *Pop the other half of the bun on top and sink your teeth into this delicious summer treat!*

### TOP TIP
Large Portobello mushrooms also go well with halloumi and are a great replacement for a meaty burger.

# REMARKABLE REPTILES

People don't often realise that there are six different species of reptile which are native to the British Isles. This is possibly because they are really rare and also really shy, so you are unlikely to come across them frequently. Most British reptiles are not poisonous. However, if you are on the lookout for reptiles, please take care and observe the guidelines below. Although the creatures are very beautiful and fascinating, you must keep yourself – and the animal you are observing – safe at all times.

1. **Take an adult with you.**

2. **Keep a safe distance at all times.**

3. **Never touch or disturb a lizard or snake.**

4. **If you are bitten, go straight to hospital and tell the doctor what the creature looked like.**

5. **Go to the NHS website to find out more https://www.nhs.uk/conditions/snake-bites**

## DID YOU KNOW...

There are no adders or grass snakes in Ireland or Northern Ireland. There is a story that St Patrick banished all snakes from the island! We now know that after the Ice Age snakes were not able to get to Ireland before it became an island.

The best time to see reptiles is in hot weather as they love to bask in the sunshine. Lizards and snakes can be found in a variety of places including sand dunes and woodland. Sometimes you might even spot one in a compost heap.

## CAN YOU SPOT...

Common lizard

Sand lizard

Slow worm

Adder

Grass snake

Smooth snake

# RAINY DAY FUN

There's nothing worse than a rainy day in the summer, is there? Well, maybe after trying one of these activities, you'll change your mind!

★ Ask for any cardboard boxes which are in the recycling pile and use them to build a town in the sitting room!

★ Put on a play or a show for your family. You could ask for some old socks to make puppets out of.

★ How about making a family magazine? Interview your family about their lives then write about them. Ask for old photos you can cut up and glue into the magazine.

★ Make cupcakes and decorate them – and then eat them. You deserve a treat on a day like this!

★ Why not visit a library and take part in the Summer Reading Challenge – choose six books to read over the summer so that you can collect all your stickers from the library.

# Make a *Sock Puppet*

Why not turn a few old socks into characters and use them to put on a puppet show. Have a think about the stories you could tell in your sock theatre before you start making the puppets. Well-known fairy tales might give you some inspiration.

Fabric glue works well for sticking on the faces and so on, but if you are good at sewing, your puppets will last longer. Remember to ask permission from the adult in your house before you start raiding the sock drawer!

## You will need:

**Old, long, clean socks of any colour (sports socks or knee socks are best)**
**Fabric glue or a needle and thread**
**Marker pens**
**Pom-poms**
**Buttons**
**Scraps of felt or other fabric**
**Wool or string**

1 *Choose your sock and make sure there aren't any huge holes in it!*

2 *Put a sock over your hand and make a C-shape with your fingers – push your fingers into the toe part and try to get your thumb into the heel part.*

3 *Open and close your hand. This is your puppet's mouth!*

4 *Use a marker pen to make two dots for the eyes. If you want your puppet to have a nose, make a dot for that as well.*

5 *Remove the sock and spread it flat on the table. The marks for the eyes and nose may look out of place, but don't worry.*

6 *Glue some eyes on to the sock or draw them on with marker pens. Add long eyelashes too if you like.*

7 *Use a small pom-pom or button for the nose, or cut a triangle or circle out of felt and use that instead.*

8 *Stick on some wool or string for hair.*

9 *Now you are ready for the opening night of your Sock Puppet Theatre!*

# CAMPING

Sleeping outdoors is one of the most fun activities for friends and family to enjoy during the warm summer months. You don't have to go away and stay on a campsite. If you have a garden, why not camp there? You can have just as much fun. And if you get a bit chilly, you can creep indoors and get back into your own bed! But after you've tried all these things, you won't want to go back inside . . .

## ❶ Go on a nature walk

Once you have pitched your tent, go for a walk as the sun is setting. Listen to all the sounds around you. Which birds can you hear? What can you see? Try to walk around as quietly as you can so that you don't frighten any of the wildlife. You might hear owls or see a badger or a fox.

## ❷ Cook over the campfire

This is the best bit about camping! Don't forget to pack a box of matches with your camping things. Then, while you are on your nature walk, gather some small, dry sticks. You can use these to start your fire. Stick a sausage on a skewer or make campfire bread by mixing flour, water and a pinch of salt into a thick dough and wrapping it around a clean stick. Then carefully hold the food over the flames until it is cooked. Marshmallows make a perfect dessert.

### ❸ Tell stories and sing songs by the fire

Once you have had enough to eat, enjoy the warmth of the fire and the way the flames flicker and make shadows. It's just the right atmosphere for having a good singalong. Or maybe, if you're feeling brave, you could get someone to tell ghost stories! Always make sure that you put out the fire completely when you are finished by pouring water over the embers. Never light a fire during periods of very dry weather as it could get out of control.

### ❹ Play torchlight tag

If you're getting a bit chilly, a game of tag will warm you up. Make sure you all have torches so that you don't trip over anything. It's fun to chase each other's torchlight in the dark!

### ❺ Look at the stars

Before you crawl into your snug sleeping bag, look up at the night sky. You will know quite a lot about the constellations by now, so see if you can spot any of the ones you have learned about in this book.

# SEPTEMBER

## SPECIAL DAYS

**15th** Rosh Hashanah (Jewish New Year)

**19th** Ganesh Chaturthi (Hindu festival)

**21st** Mabon (pagan celebration)/Harvest festival (Christian festival)

**23rd** Autumn equinox

**24th** Yom Kippur (Jewish holiday)

**27th** The Prophet's birthday (Muslim celebration)

**29th** Michaelmas Day (Christian celebration)

# ANNIVERSARIES

**95 years ago . . .**

On 28 September 1928, Sir Alexander Fleming noticed mould growing on some bacteria in his laboratory. The mould was killing the bacteria. This mould was later used in the antibiotic medicine we now call penicillin which helps to stop some infections.

**250 years ago . . .**

On 1 September 1773, the first book of poems by African American poet Phillis Wheatley was published. They helped to raise awareness of slavery and therefore played a part in ending it too. Her book was the first collection of published poetry by an African American person.

"*Every leaf speaks bliss to me*
*Fluttering from the autumn tree.*"

EMILY BRONTË (1818–1848)

September can be a golden month. Summer is fading, yes, but there is still warmth in the air, and the leaves on the trees are slowly turning from their different shades of green to the fiery colours of autumn. And, of course, the end of summer means the beginning of school again, which not everyone is happy about! But the days are still long enough to allow some time for fun in the park after school, so make the most of it before the clocks change and the countdown to winter begins.

*Phases of the Moon* **in September 2023**

| **Last Quarter** | **New Moon** | **First Quarter** | **Full Moon** |
| 6th September | 15th September | 22nd September | 29th September |

### Why is September Called September?

This month kept its original name from the Roman calendar. September comes from the Latin word *septem*, which means 'seven'. September was the seventh month of the year when the calendar began with March and only had ten months.

### Constellation of the Month

*Cygnus* means 'swan' in Latin. The Romans took the word from the Greek *kyknos*. The ancient Greeks had many stories about swans. One of them feaured the tragic hero Orpheus. He was killed and then transformed into a swan, after which he was placed in the sky. The constellation of Cygnus is quite easy to spot as it is shaped like a cross. It is also sometimes known as the Northern Cross.

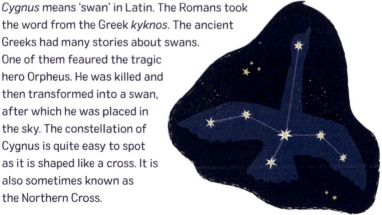

# FESTIVAL FUN

If you found it hard to stick to your New Year's resolutions, you could try starting again in September! This month is a time for new beginnings for some religions. It is also time to give thanks for nature's gift to us of the harvest.

### 15th September *Rosh Hashanah*

This is a very important Jewish festival as it celebrates the start of the New Year in the Hebrew calendar. It is one of Judaism's holiest days and begins on the first day of Tishrei, which is the seventh month in the Hebrew calendar. Rosh Hashanah is a time for giving thanks for the birth of the universe and the day on which God created Adam and Eve. The festival begins at sunset on 15th September and goes through to sunset on 17th September. People light candles, enjoy special meals and come together to pray.

### 19th September *Ganesh Chaturthi*

This is the day that Hindus start celebrating the birthday of Lord Ganesha, the god with the head of an elephant. Communities get together to worship, have parties and decorate their houses with models and pictures of Lord Ganesha. He is known as the god of new beginnings and is supposed to bring prosperity, good fortune and success.

## DID YOU KNOW...

According to some stories in Hindu mythology, the moon laughed at Ganesha for having such a large stomach. Ganesha got angry and declared that from that day, if anyone looked at the moon on Ganesh Chaturthi, they would fall over.

**21st September** *Mabon or Harvest Festival*

The harvest festival is the closest thing we have to a day of thanksgiving in Britain. The word 'harvest' comes from the Old English word *hærfest* meaning 'autumn'. This was a very important time of year, as the success of the harvest could mean the difference between life or death for a whole community. In the past, even children had to help bring in the harvest. Then, as soon as it was over, everyone would return from the fields for the harvest supper. This was a huge feast with much singing and laughter.

## Make your own *Blackberry Ink*

**You will need:**

Apron
Metal spoon
Sieve
Bowl or jug
Glass jar or small
bottle with lid

2 or 3 good handfuls
of ripe blackberries
1 teaspoon of vinegar
Calligraphy pen or
very slim paintbrush
Thick paper or card

**1** *Put the berries in the sieve over the bowl or jug.*

**2** *Using the spoon, mash the berries into a smooth pulp – the juice will go into the bowl and leave the seeds and skin of the berries in the sieve.*

**3** *Once you have all of the berry juice in the bowl, add the vinegar and mix thoroughly.*

**4** *Ask a grown-up to help you pour the ink into the jar or bottle. Wear an apron as any spilled juice will stain your clothes!*

**5** *Dip your calligraphy pen or paintbrush into the ink and use it to write your letter or paint your picture.*

**6** *Tightly screw the lid on the jar or bottle when you have finished. The ink should stay brightly coloured for a few days.*

Mabon is a pagan festival which is celebrated at the time of the autumn equinox. This is when the day is the same length as the night. It is a time for being thankful for everything nature gives us – you might want to spend some time being thankful for food that is grown in the earth, for example. Or you might want to think about all the lovely things you enjoy doing outside in nature.

It is also a time to give gifts to other people and to think of others who are less fortunate than ourselves. Perhaps you could donate some food to your local foodbank, or bake a cake for a relative or neighbour who needs cheering up. Or you could write a letter or paint a picture for someone who has done something nice for you. How about doing this with your own homemade blackberry ink?

**24th September** *Yom Kippur*

This is the holiest day of the year for Jewish people. It is a day for saying sorry for things you have done wrong and asking for forgiveness. Jewish people traditionally wear white and they fast and pray for up to 25 hours. They often spend most of the day in the synagogue.

**27th September** *The Prophet's Birthday*

In Britain and all over the world, some Muslims see this as a day to celebrate. In some countries there are street parades, the mosques are decorated and children read out poems about the Prophet's life. People can spend the day donating food and money to charity too. Other Muslims see this day as a time for concentrating on the holy book, the *Qur'an*.

**29th September** *Michaelmas Day*

The Christian celebration of Michaelmas, or the 'Feast of St Michael and All Angels' falls near the equinox. This is why most schools and universities start their new year around September; some of them even call the autumn term 'Michaelmas Term'. Traditionally, Michaelmas Day was the time when new servants were hired or land was bought or sold, and money was paid back to people who had lent it.

# CREEPY CRAWLIES

Poor old spiders have got quite a bad name for themselves – so many people are scared of them! We shouldn't be frightened of spiders in Britain, though, as they are not dangerous. In fact, they are very useful and do a lot of good.

### Six Spidery Facts

★ People think there are more spiders around in the autumn, but actually it's just that we're more likely to see them at this time of year. This is because they are now fully grown and also because it's the mating season, so the males can be seen hurrying around trying to find a female.

★ House spiders don't particularly like baths – and they definitely don't like getting wet. It's just that they sometimes fall in and then can't climb out! This is especially true of large spiders which, unlike some smaller ones, can't walk up smooth surfaces.

★ All British spiders use poison to digest their prey. However, they are very unlikely to harm humans.

★ We live alongside so many spiders that we are never more than a metre away from one! Most are very small, though, so you probably won't even see them.

★ Very few spiders enjoy living in modern centrally heated homes. Most of them would prefer us to take them back outside, as they really like living in garages or sheds where they can hide in peace and quiet.

★ You might not like having spiders around, but they are useful because they eat other bugs that we dislike, including midges and mosquitoes. So remember – things would be a lot worse if there weren't any spiders around.

**TOP TIP**
Try leaving strips of loo paper hanging into the bath to help trapped spiders climb out!

CAN YOU SPOT...

False widow

Cave spider

Money spider

Black lace-weaver

Lace-web spider

Garden spider

House spider

# YOU SAY TOMATO...

Is the tomato a fruit or a vegetable? People have been arguing about this for hundreds of years: in America in 1887 the argument went all the way to the US Supreme Court! This may sound silly, but it was quite important because if it was decided that tomatoes were vegetables, they would be more expensive.

In actual fact, the tomato is a fruit because it contains seeds and grows on a vine. The same is true of cucumbers, squashes, beans and peas. But, of course, everyone thinks of them as vegetables because they are served in savoury dishes and not as desserts!

We can get tomatoes all year round, but when growing your own, the best time to pick them is often in late August or early September. While the days are still golden and warm, it's lovely to throw your own tomatoes into a salad. As the month wears on, you might be left with a few that are not so nice to eat raw, but they are still great for soups, chutneys, stews and this delicious tomato salsa.

## Recipe for *Tangy Tomato Salsa*

Salsas are delicious with tortilla chips or as an addition to fajitas – and they are very easy to make! You'll need a grown-up to help with the chopping, but you can help with squeezing the limes and stirring everything together at the end. Then put your tasty tomato salsa in the centre of the table for everyone to enjoy as a dip – or use it to put in delicious wraps, stuffed with your favourite fillings.

**You will need:**

**Sharp knife**
**Chopping board**
**Lemon squeezer**
**Bowl**

**4–6 medium ripe tomatoes**
**Half a red onion**
**1 clove of garlic**
**1 tablespoon of white wine vinegar**
**Salt and pepper**
**1 small lime**
**Handful of fresh coriander leaves**

1 *Chop the tomatoes into tiny cubes.*

2 *Chop the onion, garlic and coriander leaves as finely as possible.*

3 *Cut the lime in half and use the squeezer to get all the juice out.*

4 *Put all the ingredients together with the vinegar into a bowl.*

5 *Mix well and serve straight away or keep in the fridge until the meal or snack is ready.*

## DID YOU KNOW...

'Salsa' is a Spanish word which means 'sauce'.

# WILD SEA, WILD ME

Believe it or not, September is the best month to go for a swim in the sea. This is because the water has been warming up over the summer and it is now as warm as it will be all year. If you do fancy a dip, take a grown-up with you and be careful to check the tides beforehand. Make sure you are swimming in a safe area where you can get in and out easily. Also, take a good look at the waves first, as the sea can begin to get quite stormy and rough in September.

# IT'S A RUBBISH GAME!

Sadly there is often a lot of litter on our beaches, but the good news is we can all do our bit to clean it up. If you don't want to join in with an organised beach clean, you can do a mini one with your family and friends – and turn it into a game to see who can pick up the most litter. This will make it more fun! Once you have taken the litter home, you'll need to sort through it and recycle what you can, and there may be some bits and bobs that you can use to make things from.

Make sure you ask a grown-up to help you and always wear gloves or use a litter-picker when you are collecting things from the beach. And remember to wash any items before you use them in your craft activities.

## DID YOU KNOW...

Making things from objects you find is sometimes known as 'upcycling'.

Why not make your own postcards? They can be used as thank you notes or just to send a message to make your friends and family smile. Draw an animal, fish or bird and use some of the litter you have found to complete your picture. You could use old Smarties lids or bottle tops for the animals' bodies or noses. Little bits of plastic from old crisp packets can be good for making fins or tails for a fish, or a whale, or even a beak for a bird. How many different sea creatures can you make from the things you find?

The end of a plastic bottle makes a perfect jellyfish's body! Use marker pens to decorate it if you like. Did you find any string or rope or long strips of plastic on the beach? If so, you could use them for the tentacles. Then make a hole in the top of the jellyfish and thread some more string through it so you can hang it up. You have made your own jellyfish mobile!

# OCTOBER

## SPECIAL DAYS

**21st** Apple Day

**29th** Daylight saving ends (clocks go back)

**31st** All Saints' Eve (Christian festival)/Halloween

# ANNIVERSARIES

**85 years ago . . .**

On 30 October 1938, the English science-fiction writer H.G. Wells broadcast a recording of his book *The War of the Worlds* on the radio in the United States. Many listeners believed that planet Earth had been invaded by aliens and a lot of people panicked!

**100 years ago . . .**

On 16 October 1923, Walt Disney started the Disney Company with his older brother Roy. They are famous for creating cartoon characters such as Mickey and Minnie Mouse, Donald Duck and Goofy, which can be seen walking around Disney theme parks all over the world, from Tokyo, Japan, to Paris, France!

> *"I'm so glad I live in a world where there are Octobers."*

L. M. MONTGOMERY (1874–1942)

October leads us gently into autumn. The days are still mild and the light is golden as it reflects off the turning leaves. The colours are glorious! This is the perfect time of year to go out walking in the countryside or in the park. Run through the fallen leaves and look out for especially beautiful colours and shapes. Maybe you could collect your favourite leaves and press them? Pressed autumn leaves make brilliant decorations on cards or bookmarks.

## DID YOU KNOW...

13th October falls on a Friday this year and some people believe that this is unlucky. This might be because of a story from Norse mythology – one day the 12 gods were having dinner when naughty Loki turned up as well and ruined the party for everyone!

## Why is October Called October?

October gets its name from the Latin word *octo* which means 'eight', and was named by the Romans during a time when the calendar year began with March instead of with January as it does now.

The Anglo-Saxon name for this month was *Winterfylleth* which comes from the words for 'winter' and 'full moon'.

## October Birth Signs

**Libra** The sign of the scales. Librans are said to have a balanced personality, and are supposed to like peace and harmony. This is the birth sign for people born between 23rd September and 23rd October.

**Scorpio** The sign of the scorpion. This is the birth sign for people born between 24th October and 21st November. They are thought to be brave, passionate and stubborn! They are also said to like the truth and have deep, long-lasting friendships.

## The Moon's a Balloon!

The October full moon is called the Hunter's Moon. It is also known as the Blood Moon because it can often be a striking red or orange colour. Of course, the colour of the actual moon hasn't changed! The moon hangs lower in the sky at this time of year, closer to the horizon, and so we are seeing it through more of the Earth's atmosphere. The gases around the Earth and the tiny particles in the air affect the way in which we see light. Orange and red light has longer wavelengths and so these are the colours we see reflected off the moon when it is closer to us.

### 31st October *All Saints' Eve*

This is a Christian festival also known as All Hallows' Eve, Hallowed Evening or Holy Evening, which is how we get the name Halloween! On the evening of 31st October, some Christians begin three days of ceremonies and services to remember loved ones who have died and the saints ('hallowed' or holy people). It is traditional to light candles for those who have died and to spend time praying and remembering them.

### 31st October *Halloween*

Nowadays, we associate Halloween with fun and games and dressing-up. But in fact, as far back as the 16th century, people had parties on 31st October, playing games and practising rituals to try and tell the future, especially about deaths or marriages in the family. This is where the game of apple-bobbing comes from. It used to be thought that the first person to bite into an apple would be the first person to get married!

Before pumpkins were brought over from America, people would use turnips or other root vegetables to make lanterns. These were carved with ugly faces in the hope that they would scare away evil spirits.

# APPLES GALORE

October is apple month! If you live in an area where there are a lot of apple trees, you might find lots of apples falling on the ground. These are known as 'windfalls'. They might look battered and bruised, but windfalls are excellent apples to put in pies, crumbles and cakes. They make delicious apple sauce as well, which is yummy as a dessert with ice cream or yoghurt and also goes very well with roast pork. Always check windfalls carefully as there are a lot of sleepy wasps around at this time of year and they can sometimes be found slowly munching their way through apples that are on the ground. You will also need to wash windfalls and cut out any bruised flesh before you use them for cooking.

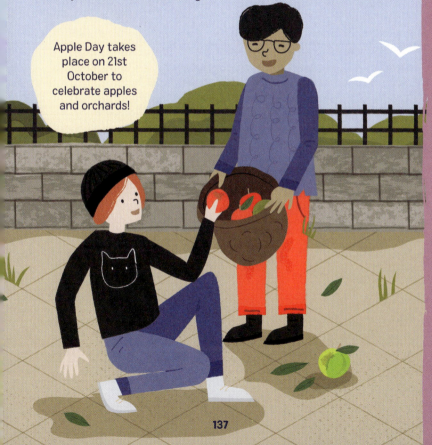

Apple Day takes place on 21st October to celebrate apples and orchards!

# Make a *Yucky Dip!*

Have you heard of a 'lucky dip' which is a game where you put your hand into a bag and pull out a prize? Well, this is a YUCKY dip! If you are having a Halloween party this is a fun thing to make and use for a game with your friends and family.

## You will need:

**Large see-through bowl or plastic container**
**Pack of orange jelly**
**Pack of purple jelly**
**Pack of green jelly**
**Packets of sweets such as jelly babies**

1. *Make the orange jelly according to the instructions.*
2. *Pour it into the see-through container and drop in some of the sweets.*
3. *Leave until the jelly has set.*
4. *Repeat the process with the purple jelly and add some more sweets.*
5. *When the purple jelly has set, finish your dip with the green jelly.*
6. *Leave in the fridge until it's time to play the game.*

The game is simple – you blindfold your guests and ask them to plunge their hand into the jelly to pull out some sweets! You might need to play this outside or put something down on the floor to protect it because it gets VERY messy! And remember to wash your hands afterwards.

# PUMPKIN CARVING

How about carving your own pumpkin lantern? These look great as table decorations for a Halloween party or you can leave them outside your house to welcome trick-or-treaters.

How scary can you make your lantern? Draw the most monstrous face you can think of on the side and then ask an adult to help you carve out the shapes!

**You will need:**

**Medium-sized pumpkin**
**Chopping board**
**Large metal spoon**
**Medium bowl**
**Biro or marker pen**
**Sharp knife**
**Tea light**

**1** *Ask an adult to help you cut a small 'lid' off the top of the pumpkin.*

**2** *Use the metal spoon to remove the seeds and scoop out as much of the flesh as you can.*

**3** *Put the flesh in a bowl and put aside.*

**4** *Draw a face on the pumpkin.*

**5** *Ask an adult to help you cut out the eyes, nose and mouth.*

**6** *Ask an adult to help you light a tea light and put it in the pumpkin.*

**7** *Ask an adult to help you place the finished pumpkin in a safe position. Turn out all the lights! Your super scary pumpkin lantern is spookily ready for Halloween!*

# BLACK HISTORY MONTH

In Britain, Black History Month is in October. It's a time for people to celebrate the contributions that black people have made to the country. The idea for Black History Month originally came from the USA and it is still celebrated there in February every year.

The American historian Carter G. Woodson came up with the idea. He had found that Americans knew a lot about the history of white people in their country, but that no one seemed to speak or write about the history of Black Americans. He wanted people to be properly educated so that Black people would no longer be discriminated against and treated badly because of the colour of their skin, so he set up the Association for the Study of Negro Life and History in 1915, which encouraged historians to research and write about Black history and culture.

*Ignatius Sancho*

*Mary Prince*

In the 1970s, a man called Akyaaba Addai-Sebo went from Britain to America and was inspired by Black History Month. He thought that Britain should be celebrating it too, so he started the British version in 1987.

Black History Month is a time for celebration and remembrance, and there are many wonderful talks, food festivals and musical events you can go to – everything that celebrates the achievements, culture and contributions from Black people to our lives today.

## DID YOU KNOW...

It is believed that Black History Month is celebrated in October in Britain because, traditionally, October is when African chiefs and leaders gather to settle their differences, so Akyaaba chose this month to reconnect with African roots.

*Mary Seacole*

*Rosa Parks*

*Martin Luther King Jr.*

# THE DARK IS RISING

The days are getting shorter and shorter. However, we still have light evenings until the clocks change in the early hours of 29th October. This means we get an extra hour in bed that morning. It can be confusing if you are a baby or a pet as it messes around with your mealtimes!

**Why Do the Clocks Change?**

We didn't always bother with changing the clocks. In the old days, people went to bed when the sun went down and got up again when it rose. Midday was several minutes earlier in the east of the country than it was in the south, and several minutes later in the west. This meant that town clocks across the British Isles showed different times. The building of the railway network changed all that because the time had to be the same all over the country, or people would not have had the faintest idea when to catch a train.

Then a man called William Willett suggested to Parliament that if the clocks changed, we would all enjoy more daylight in the autumn and winter months. So, since 1916, the clocks have gone back one hour in October and put forward by one hour in March. This is known as 'daylight saving'.

**TOP TIP**

In spring, the clocks 'spring forward' an hour, and in the autumn, they 'fall back'.

142

# TIME FOR BED

As well as migrating, autumn is a time for some birds and animals to hibernate, which means they go to sleep for the whole winter. There are not many creatures that do this in Britain, as our winters are not as cold as in other parts of the world, but hedgehogs, dormice, and bats do.

## Why Do Animals Hibernate?

It's not just because they like being warm and cosy – or lazy! Animals who hibernate aren't simply going to sleep – their bodies have adapted to make sure they survive during the winter months. When they go into hibernation, their bodies slow down so that they breathe less often, their hearts beat more slowly and their body temperature drops. As their bodies are not using as much energy as when they are awake and running around, they don't need to eat so much. However, before they hibernate they make sure they eat lots and lots so they have plenty of energy in reserve during their long winter sleep.

### TOP TIP
You can help hedgehogs in your garden by leaving out hedgehog biscuits or by growing patches of brambles for them to eat!

## Make an *Autumn Forest 'Globe'*

Everyone loves a snow globe! When you shake it and the 'snow' falls inside, it's so magical! Why not have a go at making an autumn forest version with all the beautiful leaves you can find outside at this time of the year? You could spend the whole day on this activity!

You could start by going for a walk in the park or the woods on a mild, dry morning when it's not windy. Remember to wear gloves to protect your hands, and take a bag with you for collecting the leaves. While you're walking, look on the ground for lots of different types and colours of leaves and put the best ones in your bag.

When you get home, see if you can find out which trees the leaves have come from. Then when it starts to get dark you can get cosy for the next part of the activity!

Maybe make some hot chocolate to warm you up while you lay out all your leaves on some newspaper. This will help them dry a bit if they are damp and it also helps you to see them all so you can choose which ones you want to use.

### TOP TIP

If you like you can glue some small pebbles or bits of gravel to the inside of the lid to make the 'ground' in your autumn forest. If you are feeling very creative you could make a small house from an empty matchbox or some modelling clay and stick that to the forest floor too!

**You will need:**

**Large preserving jar or
any large glass jar with a lid
Glycerine
Water
Lots of different types
of autumn leaves – smaller
leaves work better for this
activity**

1. *Fill the jar about three quarters of the way with water.*
2. *Add a few drops of glycerine – this will help the leaves float.*
3. *Add your leaves.*
4. *Screw the lid on the jar nice and tight.*
5. *Give the 'globe' a shake and watch your autumn leaves spiral and fall!*

# NOVEMBER

## SPECIAL DAYS

**1st** Samhain Eve (pagan festival)/
All Saints' Day (Christian celebration)

**2nd** All Souls' Day (Christian celebration)

**5th** Guy Fawkes Night (Bonfire Night)

**11th** Armistice Day (Remembrance Day)/Martinmas

**12th** Diwali (Hindu New Year)/Remembrance Sunday

**26th** Stir-up Sunday (last Sunday before Advent)

**30th** St Andrew's Day (Scotland)

# ANNIVERSARIES

**60 years ago . . .**

On 22 November 1963, the author C.S. Lewis died. He is famous for writing the Narnia books, which include *The Lion, the Witch and the Wardrobe.*

**60 years ago . . .**

On 23 November 1963 the first episode of *Doctor Who* was broadcast on the BBC. It is the most successful and longest-running science-fiction television series in the world.

**75 years ago . . .**

On 14 November 1948, Prince Charles (Prince of Wales) was born. He is Queen Elizabeth II's first son and is first in line to take the throne after her.

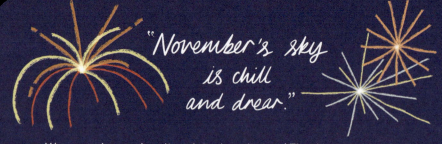

"November's sky
is chill
and drear."

We can no longer deny it – winter is on its way! The shortest day is less than two months' away, so it is no wonder that so many festivals this month celebrate light. Many festivals also focus on sweet-tasting food – a sweet treat can be just what you need when you've been outside, battling the cold! There is also all the fun of Bonfire Night to look forward to.

If your family and friends are having a bonfire for Bonfire Night, make sure you protect any curious hedgehogs who might try and burrow their way into the piles of leaves and wood. You can stop hedgehogs from doing this by building a small fence with chicken wire around the edge. And if you do find a hedgehog, put on some gardening gloves (or oven gloves) before touching its spiky little body. This is also to protect the hedgehog as they don't like getting the smell of humans on them!

*Phases of the Moon* **in November 2023**

| **Last Quarter** | **New Moon** | **First Quarter** | **Full Moon** |
|---|---|---|---|
| 5th November | 13th November | 20th November | 27th November |

### Why is November Called November?

The word 'November' comes from the Latin word for the number nine, *novem*. This is because, just like September and October before it, November keeps its name from a time when the calendar had only 10 months.

The Anglo-Saxons called this month *Blotmonath,* which means 'blood month'. This is because it was traditional at this time of year to kill farm animals and preserve the meat for the winter months ahead.

## DID YOU KNOW…

November is the only month used to represent a letter in the NATO phonetic alphabet. For example, if you wanted to spell out 'nice' you would say 'November India Charlie Echo'.

This alphabet was invented so that even if someone had a strong accent, it would be clear to the person they were speaking to which letter they wanted to use. Today, police officers use the phonetic alphabet over their radios to make sure important messages are heard clearly.

# FESTIVAL FUN

**5th November** *Guy Fawkes or Bonfire Night*

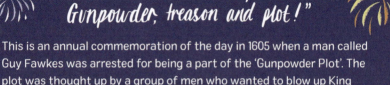

*"Remember, remember the 5ᵗʰ of November,
Gunpowder, treason and plot!"*

This is an annual commemoration of the day in 1605 when a man called Guy Fawkes was arrested for being a part of the 'Gunpowder Plot'. The plot was thought up by a group of men who wanted to blow up King James I and the Houses of Parliament in London. Guy Fawkes was found hiding beneath the House of Lords, guarding some explosives. Thankfully, the bombs never went off.

Nowadays, people spend the evening going to firework displays, standing around a big bonfire and eating hot dogs! It is a great way to chase away the winter blues.

**11th November** *Armistice Day (Remembrance Day)*

Armistice Day or Remembrance Day is a time for remembering all those who were killed in the First and Second World Wars and other wars that have since followed. A two-minute silence is held to remember the dead on the Sunday nearest to 11th November. People traditionally wear a red poppy around this time to show that they have not forgotten the people who died in the war.

## 12th November *Diwali*

Diwali marks the start of the Hindu New Year. Sikhs and Jains also celebrate at this time. Diwali is five days long, and on the third day, many Hindus light special oil lamps called *diyas*. The lamps symbolise the triumph of light over darkness, good over evil and knowledge over ignorance. Many gods, including Rama and his wife Sita, and Lakshmi, the goddess of wealth and prosperity, are celebrated with music *puja* (prayers), firework displays and by sharing traditional sweets.

## 26th November *Stir-up Sunday*

This is the last Sunday before Advent, which is the period of time in which Christians prepare for Christmas, and is the day people traditionally make their Christmas puddings. In the old days, it was a time for families to get together to mix and steam the pudding. Everyone would take a turn to stir the pudding and make a special wish for the year ahead.

## Make a *Rangoli*

Rangolis are very colourful patterns, usually inspired by nature, which are placed outside the home to celebrate the coming of the goddess Lakshmi. They are also used to welcome friends and family into the home at Diwali, and are made using geometric shapes such as triangles and ovals to create the shape of flowers or leaves.

Rangolis can be made from coloured rice, or sugar or beans, which are then stuck to card. You can also make a rangoli by drawing with coloured pens or paints – some people draw them in chalk on the pavement outside their homes. The beautiful bright colours make people think of the light that is to come after the long, dark winter is over. Why not make your own rangoli and hang it on the door to welcome your friends and family during this festival of light?

**You will need:**

**Paper plate**
**Pencil**
**Rice, beans, pasta shapes**
**Marker pens in lots of different colours**
**Glue**
**Thread or string (optional)**

1. *Draw your design on to your plate.*
2. *Choose where on your design the pasta shapes, beans and rice will go.*
3. *Colour the pasta, beans and rice with the pens, then glue them on to the design.*
4. *If you like, ask an adult to help you make a hole in the top and thread some string through so that you can hang your rangoli up in the window or on your front door.*

# OUT IN THE WILD

While we humans are busy huddling by the fire and staying warm and cosy, nature carries on working. If you have had enough of being stuck indoors, get your family out on a nature walk. Wrap up warm and keep your eyes peeled. It might be winter, but there's still lots to see!

Robins are very busy at this time of year, singing to protect their territories and finding food.

Listen out as the sun goes down and you might hear tawny owls calling to one another. The female calls out, 'Too-wit,' and the male answers her, 'Too-whoo!'

Go for a walk around a river estuary. Birds flock to these places in the winter as the water does not freeze so there is always plenty of food to be found. You might even see a kingfisher or an otter.

Foxes are out hunting in the early evening. They can often be seen slinking into hedges or scurrying down driveways just after the sun has set.

Go for a walk by the sea. This is a great time of year to search the empty beaches for treasures – shells, pebbles and seed pods can all be used to make beautiful decorations.

Walk in the woods too! Collect holly and ivy and pine cones and twigs and then come home and have fun making natural decorations for the house.

153

# THE COLOURS OF NATURE

You might think that there are not many colours around at this time of the year – after all, there are fewer flowers in bloom and most of the autumn leaves have fallen from the trees. It might look quite bleak and bare outside now – all brown and grey and boring.

Is it, though? Next time you go for a walk outside, try this activity. It might change your mind about how dull the natural world looks in winter! You can either bring your colour chart along with you and complete the activity outside or, if it's a chilly day, bring your treasures home to finish.

How many different browns, greens, greys, yellows, reds and oranges can you find?

**You will need:**

**Paint chart (free of charge from most DIY stores)
Bag or large pockets!**

(1) *Look out for any small items you can find: sticks, stones, nut shells, leaves, wild seed heads, feathers, bark and pine cones.*

(2) *Put these items carefully in your bag or pockets.*

(3) *Once you think you have enough items, find a sheltered place to stop.*

(4) *Lay the colour chart out on the ground or on a picnic table.*

(5) *Lay the items you have found next to the chart.*

(6) *Look carefully at the chart – can you match your items to the colours on it? Have you found any other colours?*

155

# Recipe for *Chocolate Sauce Pear Pudding*

This pudding is very easy to make and is always a hit on a cold winter's day. It is deliciously gooey! If you can't get fresh pears, tinned ones will work just as well.

## You will need:

Paper plate
20 cm x 30 cm shallow
ovenproof dish
Large saucepan
Whisk
Bowl
Food processor
Sieve

200 g butter, plus extra
to grease the dish
300 g caster sugar
4 eggs
75 g plain flour
50 g cocoa powder
3 pears, peeled, cored and cut in half
(or one tin, juice drained)

1. Heat the oven to 190°C/170°C fan/gas mark 5.
2. Lightly grease the ovenproof dish.
3. Put the butter in the saucepan and place over a low heat until the butter has melted.
4. Remove the butter from the heat.
5. When it is slightly cooled, mix with the sugar in the food processor.
6. Whisk the eggs in the bowl.
7. Gradually add the eggs to the butter and sugar in the food processor, mixing as you go.
8. Sieve the flour and cocoa on to the top of the egg mixture, then mix well.
9. Pour the mixture into the dish and put the pears into the chocolate batter so they are just peeking out.
10. Bake for 30 minutes or until the mixture is crusty on the surface.
11. Serve warm with cream or ice cream.

## TOP TIP
Do not allow to overcook, as the cake will become spongy and you won't get the yummy chocolate sauce effect!

# WILD WINTER WALKS

Sometimes winter walks can seem boring. The weather is not great and you trudge along through the mud, wishing you were tucked up snug indoors instead. A good idea to make walks more fun is to play games on your way. See if you can get the grown-ups to join in!

## Foxes and Hares

The aim of the game is for the 'hares' to reach an end point without being caught by the 'foxes'. You'll need three whistles and it's a good idea to wear sturdy trainers or running shoes.

### How to Play

★ Choose two people to be the hares and decide on an end point for your game. Give them each a whistle. The rest of the players are the foxes.

★ The foxes count to 100 slowly as the hares run off.

★ The fox leader blows a whistle to signal the start and the foxes race off after the hares.

★ The hares must try to outrun the foxes for as long as possible. They can hide if the foxes are catching up with them, but they must blow their whistle every minute or so to give the foxes clues as to where they are.

★ The hares try to reach the finish point without getting caught.

★ If the foxes catch the hares, they should blow hard on their whistle to signal everyone to head back to the start area.

★ Then you can start the game all over again – if you are not too out of puff!

# CELEBRATE AUTUMN!

Confetti is fun to throw in the air at celebrations or put inside balloons or a piñata for parties. However, most confetti is made of plastic or paper which then causes litter and pollution, so some people are choosing not to use it any more.

If you still like the idea of using confetti, don't worry! You can make your own beautiful multicoloured confetti which is perfectly safe for the environment and also great fun to create. It will keep for months if you put it in a Tupperware container or any box with a lid. And when it falls to the ground outside, it doesn't matter because it will biodegrade into the earth and help to make lovely soil for plants to grow in when the spring comes again!

## How to make *Leaf Confetti*

**You will need:**

**Lots of autumn leaves**
**Old newspaper**
**Large, heavy book or flower press**
**Hole punch**
**Pot with a lid**

**1** *Collect as many beautiful fallen autumn leaves in as many different colours as you can.*
**2** *To dry and flatten the leaves, first put them between sheets of newspaper and then put these between the pages of a large book or use a flower press if you have one.*
**3** *Using a hole punch, cut holes from the flattened leaves.*
**4** *Empty the hole punch and put all the little circles in a pot with a lid.*
**5** *Save them for a party or celebration!*

## TOP TIP
You can use the leaves with holes in to make cards – you could even save them until next month to make Christmas cards!

# DECEMBER

## SPECIAL DAYS

**3rd**   First Sunday of Advent (Christian celebration)

**7th**   Hanukkah begins (Jewish celebration)

**15th**   Last day of Hanukkah

**21st**   Winter solstice (start of winter)/
Midwinter/Yule (pagan celebration)

**24th**   Christmas Eve/First day of Christmas
(Christian celebration)

**25th**   Christmas Day (Christian celebration)

**26th**   Boxing Day

**31st**   New Year's Eve/Hogmanay (Scotland)

# ANNIVERSARIES

**100 years ago . . .**

On 27 December 1923, Gustave Eiffel died. He was a French engineer and architect and is best known for designing the Eiffel Tower in Paris and also the framework for the Statue of Liberty in New York City.

**100 years ago . . .**

On 31 Dec 1923, The chimes of Big Ben were broadcast on radio for the first time by the BBC.

> *"I heard a bird sing
> In the dark of December."*

OLIVER HERFORD (1863–1935)

For many of us, December means only one thing – Christmas! However, it's not the only festival being celebrated this month. There have always been lots of festivities in December because we are heading towards the shortest day of the year, or Midwinter. Try and make the most of the daylight this month. Which birds can you hear singing at dawn? Are the owls busy near you at dusk? Can you spot squirrels trying to find the nuts they buried in the early autumn? It's not only humans that are busy preparing food and gathering supplies at this time of year!

December may be the start of winter, but by the end of the month the days are already getting longer. It is because of this promise of longer, lighter days that the longest night has traditionally been a time for celebration. The dark can be sad or scary sometimes, but just think: if there was no darkness, there would be no light! This is what all the festivals this month are about: finding light in the darkness.

The one thing you may hope for and not get this month is snow. You are far more likely to get snow from February through to March in Britain.

## December Birth Signs

**Sagittarius** The sign of the centaur – a mythological creature who is half-man, half-horse. People born under the sign of Sagittarius, on or between 22nd November and 21st December, are supposed to be generous and have a great sense of humour. They can also be very impatient and will often speak first and think after!

**Capricorn** The sign of the goat (a goat with large horns and a fish tail!). This is because, in legend, Capricorn was a sea-goat. The dates for this sign are 22nd December to 19th January. People born under this sign are thought to be ambitious and disciplined, but they can also be worriers.

*Phases of the Moon* **in December 2023**

| **Last Quarter** | **New Moon** | **First Quarter** | **Full Moon** |
|---|---|---|---|
| 5th December | 12th December | 19th December | 27th December |

## Why is December Called December?

This month gets its name from the Latin word for ten, *decem*. The Anglo-Saxons called December *Ærra Geola* or the month 'before Yule'. Yule was an important winter festival and is still celebrated today by pagans. Many pagan traditions of Yule have found their way into the celebration of Christmas.

## DID YOU KNOW...

Boxing Day gets its name from a time when rich people used to put presents in boxes to give to the poor or to their servants.

# FESTIVAL FUN

There's so much festival fun this month, you could be forgiven for thinking that December is one long celebration from start to finish!

### 3rd December *First Sunday of Advent*

Advent lasts for four Sundays leading up to Christmas. Advent always begins on the Sunday that falls between 27th November and 3rd December. In churches, Christians light one candle every Sunday of Advent. It is common for people to also begin their own countdown to Christmas on 1st December with Advent calendars or Advent candles which have the numbers 1 to 24 on them.

### 7th December *Hanukkah Begins*

Sometimes spelled *Chanukah*, this Jewish festival lasts for eight days. During this time, Jewish people remember how the Second Temple in Jerusalem was dedicated to God. Hanukkah is often called the festival of lights because the holiday is celebrated with the lighting of the *menorah* candlestick. Traditional foods are served, such as potato pancakes and jam-filled doughnuts called *sufganiyot*.

### 21st December *Winter Solstice or Midwinter or Yule*

The winter solstice or midwinter falls on the shortest day of the year and has been celebrated in Britain for hundreds of years. At Yule, pagans light candles and fires, decorate their homes with evergreen plants, feast, dance and give gifts. All these things are now traditional at Christmas too.

Pagans also believe that hanging a sprig of holly near the door brings good luck and keeps away evil spirits.

Mistletoe can also be hung as a decoration and as a blessing and symbol of new life.

### Five ways to *Celebrate Midwinter*

★ Go on a walk to gather greenery for your home.
★ Light a circle of candles.
★ Tell stories around the fire or by candlelight.
★ Have a feast with your favourite food and your family and friends!
★ Write down a list of everything you have to be thankful for in the past year.

# Make your own *Ice Decorations*

Decorating your home is one of the best things about getting ready for Christmas. But how about decorating the garden as well? These sparkly ice decorations are fun and easy to make and to hang on trees or bushes outside as sparkly decorations. They won't last long unless the weather is really cold, so maybe make them to welcome guests to a Christmas party or for Christmas Day itself.

You can have fun looking for things to put inside the ice – go outside on a walk around the garden or park beforehand to collect leaves, feathers or petals. Make sure you wear gloves to do this and wash your hands when you get home.

**You will need:**

Saucers or
large jar lids
Kettle
Leaves, feathers,
petals, grass

String or wool
Boiled water left to
cool slightly
Washing-up bowl
Cold water

**1** *Put the saucer or jar lid on a flat surface and put the end of the string inside, leaving the long end hanging over the edge.*

**2** *Put leaves, feathers or petals in the middle of the saucer or lid.*

**3** *Ask a grown-up to help you pour the cooled boiled water into each saucer or lid.*

**4** *Put the saucers in the freezer compartment of the fridge or outside on a window ledge if it's going to be a really cold night!*

**5** *Leave overnight to freeze.*

**6** *In the morning put the saucers or lids in a washing-up bowl of cold water.*

**7** *Lift the ice decorations out of the saucers or lids.*

**8** *Hang them around the garden or outside your window to decorate your home.*

# Recipe for *Veggie Sausage Rolls*

These are a delicious alternative to traditional meat sausage rolls, so if you have any vegetarian friends or family members, they will be very grateful to see these at your Christmas party. Although you might have to make extra, as they are so tasty everyone will want one!

## You will need:

| | |
|---|---|
| Food processor | 200 g mushrooms |
| Sharp knife | 3 tablespoons of rapeseed or olive oil |
| Chopping board | 2 leeks |
| Frying pan | 2 cloves of garlic |
| Mixing bowl | 1 tablespoon of dried sage leaves |
| Wooden spoon | 1 tablespoon of brown miso paste |
| Metal spoon | 2 teaspoons of French mustard |
| Fork | 30 g pre-cooked chestnuts |
| Baking parchment | 60 g cheddar cheese, grated |
| Baking sheet | 70 g fresh white breadcrumbs |
| Pastry brush | 1 x 320 g sheet of puff pastry |
| | 1 egg |

168

1. Pre-heat the oven to 200°C/180°C fan/gas mark 6.
2. Finely chop the leeks and garlic.
3. Put the leeks in the frying pan with the oil and fry gently until soft.
4. Put the leeks in the mixing bowl to cool – keep the pan to one side.
5. Put the mushrooms In the food processor and whizz into tiny pieces.
6. Fry the mushrooms in the pan with the garlic, sage and miso.
7. Add this mixture to the leeks in the bowl.
8. Add the mustard, cheese and breadcrumbs.
9. Whizz up the chestnuts in the food processor and add them to the bowl.
10. Use the wooden spoon to mix everything together into a thick paste.
11. Line the baking sheet with the parchment.
12. Lay the puff pastry on the baking sheet.
13. Use the metal spoon to put the veggie mixture in a long sausage shape down the middle of the pastry.
14. Pinch the edges of the pastry together around the mixture.
15. Cut into eight sausage rolls and prick them with the fork.
16. Beat the egg and brush it over the pastry.
17. Cook for 25–30 minutes until the rolls are golden brown.

## 25th December *Christmas Day*

The word Christmas comes from the Anglo-Saxon words *Cristes Mæsse*. It is the Christian celebration of the birth of Jesus Christ. In fact, his birth date is unknown. However, Christians wanted a day to celebrate their belief that Jesus brought goodness and light into the world. As there were already 'light festivals' at this time of year, such as Yule, it made sense to have Christmas then as well.

*Saturnalia* is an ancient Roman festival that probably influenced how and when Christmas is celebrated. It was dedicated to the god Saturn. All work and business stopped during the festival, and slaves were given a few days of freedom. People said *'Lo Saturnalia!'* to each other the way people today might say 'Happy Christmas!' or 'Happy Hanukkah!' At the end of the festival people would make presents of candles to one another or wax models of fruit.

## 31st December *New Year's Eve or Hogmanay*

It is the last day of the year! Just before midnight, it is traditional to turn on a radio or television to follow the countdown of the last few seconds of the old year and to watch the display of fireworks over the River Thames in London. At this point, people often hug and kiss and start to sing the song 'Auld Lang Syne' – although they often don't know the words! Here they are so that you can sing them this year:

> "Should auld acquaintance be forgot,
> and never brought to mind?
> Should auld acquaintance be forgot
> and auld lang syne?
> For auld lang syne my dear,
> for auld lang syne.
> We'll tak'a cup o' kindness yet,
> for auld lang syne."

The words were written by the Scottish poet Robert Burns in 1788. The song asks if it's right to forget old friends and things that have happened in the past.

## DID YOU KNOW...

In England and Scotland, New Year's Day used to be 25th March. Scotland made 1st January New Year's Day in 1660 and England followed in 1752.

## Just After Midnight ...

In Scotland, New Year's Eve is known as Hogmanay. If you're lucky enough to be in Scotland on 31st December (and you're allowed to stay up on New Year's Eve until after midnight!) you might be able to join in with the tradition of first-footing.

The 'first foot' to come in through the front door after the last stroke of midnight is supposed to bring good luck. The 'first-footer' should be carrying a piece of coal, some bread, salt and a small drink (known as a 'wee dram'). These items are thought to bring warmth, good food, long life and good cheer for the year ahead.

# Recipe for *Mini Christmas Cakes*

## You will need:

8 150 ml ramekin dishes
Pencil
Baking parchment
Scissors
Mixing bowl
Wooden spoon
Baking sheet
Round-edged knife
Wire rack
Small saucepan
Pastry brush
Rolling pin

## For the cake mix:

200 g butter plus a
little extra for greasing
200 g dark muscovado
sugar
3 eggs, beaten
1 tablespoon of
black treacle
200 g self-raising flour
2 teaspoons of mixed spice
1 teaspoon of baking
powder
2 medium apples
300 g mixed dried fruit

## For the decoration:

2 tablespoons of
apricot jam
500 g packet of marzipan
(contains nuts)
500 g ready-made
white icing
16 glacé cherries
Red or gold ribbon

These are a lovely present to make for someone who lives alone. A big Christmas cake might be too much for them, but these mini ones are perfect to enjoy with a cup of tea. This recipe makes enough mini cakes for you to share them and still have some yourself!

1. *Pre-heat the oven to 180°C/160°C fan/ gas mark 6.*
2. *Put the ramekins on the baking parchment and draw around the base with the pencil.*
3. *Cut the circles out.*
4. *Grease the insides of the ramekins.*
5. *Put a paper circle in the bottom of each ramekin.*
6. *Mix together all the cake mix ingredients.*
7. *Divide the mixture between the ramekins.*
8. *Put them on the baking sheet and bake for 30 minutes.*
9. *Leave them on the wire rack to cool.*
10. *Once they are completely cool, use the knife to ease the cakes gently out of the ramekins.*
11. *Slice off the tops of the cakes to make them flat.*
12. *Melt the jam in the saucepan over a gentle heat and brush it over the cakes.*
13. *Roll out the marzipan and the icing and divide them both into eight sections.*
14. *Cover the cakes with the marzipan first and then the icing.*
15. *Stick a glacé cherry on the top of each cake and tie some ribbon around them.*

# VISIT A LONELY NEIGHBOUR

Christmas is fun if you have everyone you love around the table and can enjoy playing games and spending a cosy time together. However, some people are not so fond of this time of year and can end up feeling very lonely while everyone else is gathering to celebrate.

Maybe you know someone who lives on their own and might appreciate a visit this Christmas? You could ask if you and a parent or guardian could take them one of your mini Christmas cakes. Or maybe they could come round to your home for a cup of tea with you and your family?

# WRAPPING UP THE YEAR

" There is a time for everything, and a season for every activity under the heavens."

ECCLESIASTES 3, FOUND IN THE HEBREW *TANAKH* AND THE BIBLE

So it's time to say goodbye to the old and make way for the new. Maybe you'll make those New Year's resolutions all over again . . . and just maybe you'll do better at keeping them in 2024! Whatever you do, and wherever you are, thank you for reading this book and

# HAPPY NEW YEAR TO YOU AND YOUR FRIENDS AND FAMILY!

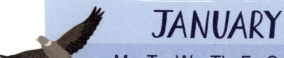
# CALENDAR 2023

## JANUARY

| Mo | Tu | We | Th | Fr | Sa | Su |
|----|----|----|----|----|----|----|
|    |    |    |    |    |    | 1  |
| 2  | 3  | 4  | 5  | 6  | 7  | 8  |
| 9  | 10 | 11 | 12 | 13 | 14 | 15 |
| 16 | 17 | 18 | 19 | 20 | 21 | 22 |
| 23 | 24 | 25 | 26 | 27 | 28 | 29 |
| 30 | 31 |    |    |    |    |    |

**Phases of the Moon**

6:◯  15:◑  21:●  28:◐

## FEBRUARY

| Mo | Tu | We | Th | Fr | Sa | Su |
|----|----|----|----|----|----|----|
|    |    | 1  | 2  | 3  | 4  | 5  |
| 6  | 7  | 8  | 9  | 10 | 11 | 12 |
| 13 | 14 | 15 | 16 | 17 | 18 | 19 |
| 20 | 21 | 22 | 23 | 24 | 25 | 26 |
| 27 | 28 |    |    |    |    |    |

**Phases of the Moon**

5:◯  13:◐  20:●  27:◑

174

# MARCH

| Mo | Tu | We | Th | Fr | Sa | Su |
|----|----|----|----|----|----|----|
|    |    | 1  | 2  | 3  | 4  | 5  |
| 6  | 7  | 8  | 9  | 10 | 11 | 12 |
| 13 | 14 | 15 | 16 | 17 | 18 | 19 |
| 20 | 21 | 22 | 23 | 24 | 25 | 26 |
| 27 | 28 | 29 | 30 | 31 |    |    |

**Phases of the Moon**

7: ○  15: ◑  21: ●  29: ◑

# APRIL

| Mo | Tu | We | Th | Fr | Sa | Su |
|----|----|----|----|----|----|----|
|    |    |    |    |    | 1  | 2  |
| 3  | 4  | 5  | 6  | 7  | 8  | 9  |
| 10 | 11 | 12 | 13 | 14 | 15 | 16 |
| 17 | 18 | 19 | 20 | 21 | 22 | 23 |
| 24 | 25 | 26 | 27 | 28 | 29 | 30 |

**Phases of the Moon**

6: ○  13: ◐  20: ●  27: ◑

# MAY

| Mo | Tu | We | Th | Fr | Sa | Su |
|----|----|----|----|----|----|----|
| 1  | 2  | 3  | 4  | 5  | 6  | 7  |
| 8  | 9  | 10 | 11 | 12 | 13 | 14 |
| 15 | 16 | 17 | 18 | 19 | 20 | 21 |
| 22 | 23 | 24 | 25 | 26 | 27 | 28 |
| 29 | 30 | 31 |    |    |    |    |

**Phases of the Moon**

5: ○   12: ◑   19: ●   27: ◐

# JUNE

| Mo | Tu | We | Th | Fr | Sa | Su |
|----|----|----|----|----|----|----|
|    |    |    | 1  | 2  | 3  | 4  |
| 5  | 6  | 7  | 8  | 9  | 10 | 11 |
| 12 | 13 | 14 | 15 | 16 | 17 | 18 |
| 19 | 20 | 21 | 22 | 23 | 24 | 25 |
| 26 | 27 | 28 | 29 | 30 |    |    |

**Phases of the Moon**

4: ○   10: ◑   18: ●   26: ◐

# JULY

| Mo | Tu | We | Th | Fr | Sa | Su |
|----|----|----|----|----|----|----|
|    |    |    |    |    | 1  | 2  |
| 3  | 4  | 5  | 6  | 7  | 8  | 9  |
| 10 | 11 | 12 | 13 | 14 | 15 | 16 |
| 17 | 18 | 19 | 20 | 21 | 22 | 23 |
| 24 | 25 | 26 | 27 | 28 | 29 | 30 |
| 31 |    |    |    |    |    |    |

**Phases of the Moon**

3: ◯  10: ◑  17: ●  25: ◖

# AUGUST

| Mo | Tu | We | Th | Fr | Sa | Su |
|----|----|----|----|----|----|----|
|    | 1  | 2  | 3  | 4  | 5  | 6  |
| 7  | 8  | 9  | 10 | 11 | 12 | 13 |
| 14 | 15 | 16 | 17 | 18 | 19 | 20 |
| 21 | 22 | 23 | 24 | 25 | 26 | 27 |
| 28 | 29 | 30 | 31 |    |    |    |

**Phases of the Moon**

1: ◯  8: ◑  16: ●  24: ◖  31: ◯

# SEPTEMBER

| Mo | Tu | We | Th | Fr | Sa | Su |
|----|----|----|----|----|----|----|
|    |    |    |    | 1  | 2  | 3  |
| 4  | 5  | 6  | 7  | 8  | 9  | 10 |
| 11 | 12 | 13 | 14 | 15 | 16 | 17 |
| 18 | 19 | 20 | 21 | 22 | 23 | 24 |
| 25 | 26 | 27 | 28 | 29 | 30 |    |

**Phases of the Moon**

6: ◐　15: ● 　22: ◑　29: ○

# OCTOBER

| Mo | Tu | We | Th | Fr | Sa | Su |
|----|----|----|----|----|----|----|
|    |    |    |    |    |    | 1  |
| 2  | 3  | 4  | 5  | 6  | 7  | 8  |
| 9  | 10 | 11 | 12 | 13 | 14 | 15 |
| 16 | 17 | 18 | 19 | 20 | 21 | 22 |
| 23 | 24 | 25 | 26 | 27 | 28 | 29 |
| 30 | 31 |    |    |    |    |    |

**Phases of the Moon**

6: ◐　14: ● 　22: ◑　28: ○

# NOVEMBER

| Mo | Tu | We | Th | Fr | Sa | Su |
|----|----|----|----|----|----|----|
|    |    | 1  | 2  | 3  | 4  | 5  |
| 6  | 7  | 8  | 9  | 10 | 11 | 12 |
| 13 | 14 | 15 | 16 | 17 | 18 | 19 |
| 20 | 21 | 22 | 23 | 24 | 25 | 26 |
| 27 | 28 | 29 | 30 |    |    |    |

**Phases of the Moon**

5:  13:  20:  27:

# DECEMBER

| Mo | Tu | We | Th | Fr | Sa | Su |
|----|----|----|----|----|----|----|
|    |    |    |    | 1  | 2  | 3  |
| 4  | 5  | 6  | 7  | 8  | 9  | 10 |
| 11 | 12 | 13 | 14 | 15 | 16 | 17 |
| 18 | 19 | 20 | 21 | 22 | 23 | 24 |
| 25 | 26 | 27 | 28 | 29 | 30 | 31 |

**Phases of the Moon**

5:  12:  19:  27:

# NOTES

# GLOSSARY

**Advent** The period leading up to Christmas

**All Saints' Eve** A Christian festival to remember saints and loved ones who have died

**Allah** The name of God for Muslims and Arab Christians

**Anglo-Saxons** People who lived in Great Britain from 410 until 1066

**Apple Day** A celebration of apples and orchards

**April Fool's Day** The first day of April, when people play jokes on each other

**Ascension Day** A Christian holy day to celebrate the day Jesus rose into heaven

**Ash Wednesday** The beginning of Lent

**Beltane** An ancient pagan festival that celebrates the return of summer

**Bible** The Christian holy book

**Birth flower** A flower linked to the month of a person's birth

**Birthstone** A precious or semi-precious stone linked to the month of a person's birth

**Blue moon** A second full moon in a calendar month

**Burns Night** A celebration of the Scottish poet Robert Burns

**Cabinet** A group of the most senior, or important, ministers in a government

**Candlemas** A Christian festival celebrating the first time that baby Jesus was taken to the temple

**Catholic** Someone who follows a branch of Christianity led by the Pope

**Chinese New Year** A colourful celebration of the start of the Chinese year, also known as the 'Spring Festival'

**Christian** Someone who follows the religion of Christianity and believes in God, Jesus Christ and the teachings of the *Bible*

**Confetti** Small pieces of paper traditionally thrown over the bride and groom at their wedding

**Dairy** Foods made from milk, including butter and cheese

**Diwali** A Hindu festival of lights to celebrate the victory of light over darkness

**Easter** A Christian festival to remember the death and return to life of Jesus Christ

**Eid al-Adha** Also known as the 'Sacrifice Feast', this Islamic festival honours Ibrahim's willingness to obey Allah and marks the end of the *Hajj* pilgrimage to Mecca

**Eid al-Fitr** Also known as the 'Festival of the Breaking of the Fast', this Islamic festival is a three-day celebration to mark the end of Ramadan

**Epiphany** A Christian holy day, held in January, which marks the end of the Christmas period

**Equator** An imaginary line drawn around the middle of the Earth at an equal distance from the north and south poles

**Equinox** The time twice a year when the length of day and night is exactly equal

**Eta Aquariids** A meteor shower formed by particles of dust left behind by Halley's Comet

**Fast** To spend a period of time without eating or drinking

**Fertility** The ability to create children or young

**First-footing** A Scottish New Year's tradition, where the 'first footer' is the first person to walk through the door after midnight

**First quarter** One quarter of the way through the moon's cycle, when we can see exactly half of the moon's face

**Fossil** The remains or traces of an ancient living thing that has been preserved in rock

**Full moon** When the entire face of the moon is lit up by the sun's rays

**Ganesh Chaturthi** A 10-day Hindu festival to worship the god Ganesha

**Guy Fawkes** A member of a group of English Catholics who tried to assassinate King James in 1604 by blowing up the Houses of Parliament

**Hanukkah** An eight-day 'festival of lights' celebrated by Jewish people, to remember how the Jewish army freed Jerusalem and took back the temple, which they re-dedicated to God

**Harvest** Gathering crops

**Hemisphere** Half of the Earth, divided into northern and southern hemispheres by the equator

**Hieroglyphics** The pictures and symbols that make up ancient Egyptian writing

**Hobby horse** A toy with a model of a horse's head at the end of a stick

**Hogmanay** The Scottish word for the last day of the year

**Holi** A Hindu spring festival in celebration of the god Krishna

**Holy Spirit** Christians believe God exists in three forms at the same time, as God in heaven, as Jesus Christ in heaven, and as the Holy Spirit, which is everywhere

**House of Commons** The British parliament, whose elected members make or change the country's laws

**Imbolc** A pagan festival marking the beginning of spring

**Isra and Mi'raj** An Islamic celebration of the Prophet Muhammad's journey from Mecca to Jerusalem and his journey into heaven, when Allah revealed to Muhammad that Muslims should pray five times a day

**Jain** Someone who follows the ancient Indian religion of Jainism that teaches *ahimsa* (non-violence) to all living creatures

**Jerusalem** The capital city of Israel, believed to be holy by Jewish people, Christians and Muslims

**Jewish people** Someone who follows the religion of Judaism and believes in God, the Hebrew prophets and the teachings of the *Torah*

**Lammas** A pagan celebration of the first harvest

**Last quarter** Three quarters of the way through the moon's cycle, when we can see exactly half of the moon's face

**Lent** A Christian period of fasting in the run-up to Easter

**LGBT+** Lesbian, gay, bisexual, transgender plus any other sexual and gender identities

**Litha** The Anglo-Saxon word for midsummer

**Lohri** A Punjabi midwinter festival celebrated by Sikhs and Hindus

**Lughnasadh** A Gaelic festival celebrating the beginning of the harvest season

**Maia** The Greek goddess of fertility

**May Day** The first day of May, celebrated by dancing and singing

**Mecca** The holiest city of Islam

**Meteor** A fiery streak in the sky, created when dust and rocks from the tail of a comet pass through the Earth's atmosphere

**Michaelmas** A Christian festival held at the end of September to honour the angels

**Midsummer** The longest day and the shortest night of the year, also known as the summer solstice

**Midwinter** The shortest day and the longest night of the year, also known as the winter solstice

**Migrate** To move from one place to another

**Mosque** The Islamic place of worship

**Muhammad** The Muslim Prophet and founder of Islam

**Muslim** Someone who follows the religion of Islam and believes in Allah, the Prophet Muhammad, the five pillars of Islam and the teachings of the *Qur'an*

**Natural remedy** A medicine made using ingredients from nature

**Neap tide** A tide that happens twice a month, when the difference between high tide and low tide is at its lowest

**New moon** The first phase in the moon's cycle, when just a very thin crescent shape is visible at night

**New Year's Honours** The titles given to people by the Queen at New Year

**Nymph** The young, or larva, of some insects such as dragonflies

**Old Testament** The first part of the *Bible*, originally written in Hebrew

**Ostara** A pagan festival which is celebrated at the spring equinox

**Pagan** A follower of paganism, a pre-Christian religion, who believes in many gods and goddesses

**Passover** A Jewish celebration to remember how Moses helped the Israelites escape from Egypt

**Pentecost** A Christian festival on the seventh Sunday after Easter, to celebrate the day after his death when Jesus returned to his disciples in the form of the Holy Spirit

**Promised Land** The land that Jewish people believe was given by God to Abraham and his descendants

**Purification** The process of making something or someone clean

**Purim** A Jewish holiday in memory of when the Jewish people were saved from a cruel man called Haman

**Qur'an** The Islamic holy book

**Raksha Bandhan** A Hindu festival that celebrates the relationship between brothers and sisters

**Ramadan** A month when Muslims hold a fast during the hours of daylight to become closer to Allah, and to remember the time that the *Qur'an* was first revealed to the Prophet Muhammad

**Resolution** A decision to do, or not do something

**Samhain Eve** A pagan festival for giving thanks at the end of the harvest

**Sea Sunday** The day when Christians pray for sailors and their families

**Shavuot** A Jewish holiday to remember the day that God gave Moses the *Torah*

**Shrove Tuesday** The day before the Christian period of fasting called Lent begins, also known as 'Pancake Day'

**Sikh** Someone who follows the religion of Sikhism and believes in the writings and teachings of the Ten Sikh Gurus

**Spring tide** A tide just after a new or full moon, when the difference between high tide and low tide is at its highest

**Sterilised** Completely clean and free from germs. You can sterilise jam jars by washing them in hot, soapy water, or by heating them in the oven at 130°C for 20 minutes (ask an adult to help you)

**Swan Upping** An annual ceremony in which mute swans are taken from the River Thames to be counted and marked to identify them, before being released

**Synagogue** The Jewish place of worship

**Ten Commandments** A list of laws or rules that Christians and Jewish people follow that they believe were given by God to Moses

**Tide** The rising and falling of the sea

**Torah** The Jewish holy book

**Trooping the colour** A ceremony performed to celebrate the Queen's birthday

**Tu B'Shevat** Jewish New Year, also known as the 'New Year for Trees'

**Twelfth Night** A festival some Christians celebrate to mark the coming of the Epiphany

**Wassailing** A pagan tradition of blessing the apple trees in the new year

**Whitsun** Another name for the Christian festival of Pentecost

**Yom Kippur** A Jewish holiday for saying sorry for things you have done wrong and asking for forgiveness

**Yule** A pagan festival held in midwinter to celebrate the winter solstice

# INDEX